The
Leopard
Gecko

An Owner's Guide To

A HAPPY HEALTHY PET

Howell Book House

IDG Books Worldwide, Inc.
An International Data Group Company
Foster City, CA • Chicago, IL • Indianapolis, IN • New York, NY

Howell Book House
IDG Books Worldwide, Inc.
An International Data Group Company
919 E. Hillsdale Boulevard
Suite 400
Foster City, CA 94404

For general information on IDG Books Worldwide's books in the U.S., please call our Consumer Customer Service department at 800-762-2974. For reseller information, including discounts and premium sales, please call our Reseller Customer Service department at 800-434-3422.

Puente, Lyle.
    The leopard gecko: an owner's guide to a happy healthy pet/Lyle Puente.
    p. cm.
    Includes bibliographical references (p. 119)
    ISBN 1-58245-165-6
    I. Leopard geckos as pets. 1. Title.
    SF 459.G35 P84 2000
    639.3'95—dc21   99-087998

Manufactured in the United States of America
10 9 8 7 6 5 4 3 2 1

Series Director: Susanna Thomas
Book Design by Michele Laseau
Cover Design by Iris Jeromnimon
External Features Illustration by Steve Adams
Photography
    Front and back covers by Bill Love
    All photography by Bill Love unless otherwise indicated
Production Team: Stephanie Lucas, Heather Pope and Linda Quigley

Contents

Welcome
to the
World

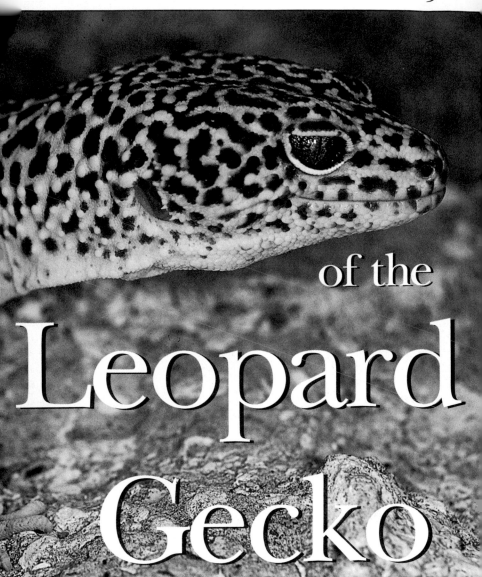

of the

Leopard

Gecko

External Features of the Leopard Gecko

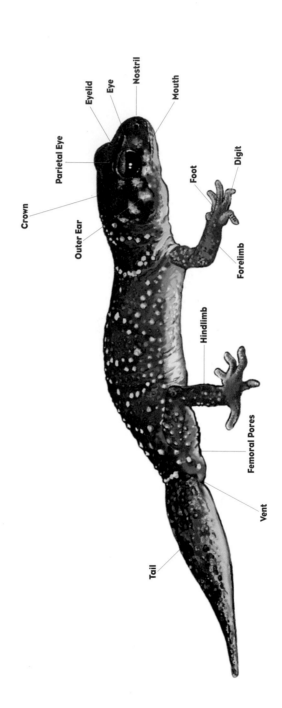

Crown

Parietal Eye

Outer Ear

Eyelid

Eye

Nostril

Mouth

Foot

Digit

Forelimb

Hindlimb

Femoral Pores

Vent

Tail

chapter 1

What Is a Leopard Gecko?

With Audrey Pavia

Geckos are an incredibly diverse and successful group of lizards. Geckos exist in many types of habitats around the world, ranging from the searing, dry desert to lush, cool mountain forests. There are many different types of geckos. The most exciting thing about geckos is their diversity. Some are unique, odd creatures. Some are virtual living jewels.

Geckos have been successful in colonizing the globe due to their ability to adapt to and exploit many types of habitats. Many gecko species have adapted to highly specialized surroundings, which are called micro habitats. One species of gecko, like a Southern African Rhotropus species, can live exclusively in rock cracks, while another species stays exclusively on the ground. Both species inhabit the same location, each exploiting specific micro habitats. This diversity in micro habitat enables many different species to share a relatively small area without interfering or competing with each other. Each species has its own niche. In areas where insects are numerous, you may find many gecko species sharing the same habitat. Each species exploits its own special micro habitat without interfering with what would seem like a natural competitor.

Other geckos have adapted to highly specialized environments. The web footed gecko (*Palmatogecko rangei*) lives on shifting sand dunes. This species has adapted to life on sand by developing webbed feet, much like duck feet. The webbing allows them to maintain traction on easily displaced sand. An arboreal gecko that is used to climbing branches would have a very difficult time on loose sand. Another terrestrial gecko with narrow toes would also have a difficult time.

The native habitat of the leopard gecko is dry and rocky.

Leaf tailed geckos (*Uroplatus* species) of Madagascar live on trees, blending in perfectly with the surrounding bark. They will remain motionless, head facing downwards, on a tree trunk. Their skin, imitating moss in one species (*Uroplatus sikkorea*), makes them seem invisible. As a prey insect wanders by the gecko can drop and quickly pounce on it. The flat leaflike tail serves as a rudder while leaping to safety. Another species, *Uroplatus phantasticus*, the satanic leaf tailed gecko, will sit motionless all day with its tail over its face and its legs out stiff and strait, imitating a dead branch.

The Leopard Gecko's Natural Habitat

The landscape of the leopard gecko is dry and rocky. Its native habitat is Pakistan, India and Afghanistan. Leopard geckos are terrestrial geckos. They live on and under the ground. They rarely climb, and when they do they can be somewhat clumsy.

THE LEOPARD GECKO'S ADAPTATIONS TO ITS HABITAT

A common misconception about geckos is that they all have sticky feet and can climb on any type of surface. Some geckos do have adhesive lamellae, which are what allow them to climb walls and glass. Leopard geckos never developed the adhesive lamellae on their toes. Because their natural habitat is dry and rocky, lamellae on their feet might make traveling difficult or hamper digging.

The leopard gecko has developed a large tail, in which the gecko is able to store fat. In a harsh climate in which food can come in hoards and then disappear for weeks, a fat-storage system can be lifesaving. A healthy leopard gecko will always have a chunky tail.

The skin of a leopard gecko is heavily patterned. Patterning in nature breaks up shapes, which helps protect and conceal the gecko from predators. The texture of the leopard gecko's skin is also bumpy, perhaps allowing it to avoid detection even better.

In the home terrarium the colors and patterns make for an unusually attractive pet. Even the blandest of leopard geckos is a stunning animal.

With these adaptations, leopard geckos are very suitable animals for captive care. They are hardy, prolific, gentle and attractive. It is no wonder hobbyists often refer to them as the perfect reptile pet.

Gecko Details

You've probably noticed that geckos look somewhat different from other lizards. This is because they have several distinctive traits.

Geckos have triangular-shaped heads and distinct necks. (African fat-tailed geckos)

HEAD

Some geckos have adhesive pads on their feet to help them climb. (tokay gecko)

One of the easiest traits to spot is the construction of their head. Geckos tend to have a triangular-shaped head, while most other lizards have a more stream-lined, V-shaped head. The other lizards' heads seem to flow right into their body. Geckos, however, usually have a discernible neck that attaches their unusual head to their body.

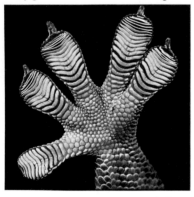

FEET

The feet of many geckos have adhesive pads on their bottoms that allow the gecko to stick to just about any surface. Not all geckos have these pads, but the ones that do can hold on pretty tight when they want to—even when they are upside down.

TAIL

One of the gecko's most distinctive characteristics is its tail. Rather than being long and narrow as on other lizards, a gecko's tail is usually narrow at the base, thick in the middle and narrow at the tip. Unlike other lizards, many geckos use their tails to store fat for those times when food might be scarce. But just like other lizards, geckos are *autotomous*. That means they can detach their tails to distract predators. The detached tail will wiggle and writhe, keeping the predator from noticing that the best part of the meal is getting away.

The gecko's autotomous nature is one reason why it's so important to handle geckos carefully: Their tails are easily detached when they are roughly handled, even by well-meaning humans.

VOICE

Many gecko species are able to vocalize. Of those that can, the male gecko uses its voice to warn away intruders to its territory and also to attract a mate; the female can also produce sounds. This makes geckos a somewhat unique family in the lizard world because most other lizards are relatively silent.

In the daylight, nocturnal geckos' pupils appear to be vertical slits; at night their pupils dilate to encompass nearly the entire eye. (Uroplatus lineatus)

EYES

The eyes of the gecko vary depending on the species. Most geckos are nocturnal (active mostly at night) and so have pupils that look like vertical slits when viewed in the daylight. These nocturnal geckos have very strong night vision, and their pupils will dilate to encompass nearly the entire eye. A few geckos are diurnal, meaning that they are most active during the day. These geckos have round pupils that look somewhat like ours.

The majority of gecko species don't have eyelids, which makes them similar to most other reptiles. However, some species of geckos—such as the leopard gecko—do have eye lids.

All geckos actually lick their eyeballs with their tongue. While scientists aren't completely sure why they do this, many suspect this is the gecko's way of keeping the eye area clean.

EARS

Gecko ears are another fascinating part of the lizard's anatomy. If you hold certain gecko species up to the light, you can actually see through their ear canals out to the other side! But don't let that fool you into thinking that there is not much in there. The gecko ear is complicated, and geckos can hear better than most other lizards. Geckos need good hearing to be able to effectively communicate with members of their own species. It's also possible that they use their hearing when hunting for prey.

REPTILE SENSES

Although lizards and snakes are classified together in the superorder Squamata, their sensory abilities are quite different. Lizards, including geckos, have a well-developed sense of taste. Along with the ability to taste with their tongues, most lizards have what is known as a Jacobson's organ in their mouths. This feature, which they share with snakes, enables them to sense chemical traces in the environment. It almost provides them with a "sixth sense." Snakes rely very heavily on the information received through their Jacobson's organ, in large part because they have quite poor vision. They need the "extra sensors" to locate food. Lizards, in contrast, have good vision, and a strong sense of taste in their tongues. They also have the ability to hear quite well; whereas snakes are essentially deaf.

ENDOLYMPHATIC SACS

Some species of geckos in the *Gekkoninae* genus have large sacs on either side of their necks. These sacs are actually reservoirs for calcium. Scientists aren't sure why some geckos have these bulging sacs, but they surmise it could be to help female geckos form egg shells, or to help in the metabolism of calcium.

DIET

One characteristic that all geckos share is a penchant for eating bugs. Without exception, all gecko species are insectivores, but some will eat other foods as well. tokay geckos, for example, have been known to drink nectar as an occasional treat. Larger species will also eat small mammals, such as newborn mice.

Other Reptilian Traits

Despite all their differences, there are many traits that geckos have in common with their reptilian cousins.

BODY TEMPERATURE

Geckos, like all reptiles, are ectothermic, which means that they are unable to internally regulate their own body temperatures the way that mammals can. Instead, geckos rely on outside sources to stay warm or cool, and must move from place to place to keep their body temperatures just right. In the early morning, a gecko will seek a warm sunlit place to heat up its body. Once the sun becomes too hot, however, the gecko will move to a shady area so its body temperature can cool down.

Geckos use their long, broad tongues to "taste" or determine the nature of things in their environment. (four spot or peacock Madagascan day gecko)

TASTE AND SMELL

Like other lizards, geckos use their tongues to "taste" things in their environment. Their long, broad tongues reach out to pick up molecules in the air.

These molecules are brought back into the mouth where they come into contact with the Jacobson's organ, located in the palate. This organ enables the gecko to determine the exact nature of whatever it is the gecko has tasted—whether it be an unrecognized insect, an obstacle in its path or your hand.

SKIN

Geckos and other lizards have an outer layer of skin made up of keratin. This layer is shed in patches as the gecko grows. They also have an inner layer of skin that contains a large number of blood vessels. Both layers of skin are very delicate and tear easily.

chapter 2

The History of Geckos

By Audrey Pavia

The natural history of the gecko is fascinating, and it takes us back to nearly the very beginning of life itself. The direct ancestor of today's gecko is the early reptile, which appeared nearly 300 million years ago, according to fossil records. Since that time, nearly all the life we see on Earth today evolved from these first reptiles—including ourselves.

When the ancestors of our pet geckos first began to walk the earth, the planet was very different than it is now. The geologic time period known as the Carboniferous Period, which occurred within the Paleozoic Era, represents a still relatively young Earth with a warm, moist climate. Giant plants reached up toward the sun, and huge insects filled the air. It was in this environment that the first reptiles evolved from amphibians, creatures that had crawled from the sea.

13

The Age of the Reptile

The very first reptiles that have been identified as such were creatures called Cotylosaurs. These ancestors of the gecko and other lizards measured around 3⅓ feet long and had short necks, stubby legs and very long tails.

A million or so years later, the earth began to cool somewhat, and the Permian Period began. The continents began to develop, the atmosphere and the oceans began to cool, and the air became somewhat drier. The insects got smaller and reptiles began to prosper. (It's interesting to note that reptiles have been feeding on insects since the Carboniferous Period, something all geckos still do today.)

Ancestors of today's geckos became prevalent in the Mesozoic Era. (Japanese leopard gecko)

It wasn't until the Mesozoic Era, also known as the Age of Reptiles, that the ancestors of today's geckos became prevalent all over the Earth. Dinosaurs began evolving from early reptiles during the Triassic Period of the Mesozoic Era, as did the first early mammals. A few million years later, during the Jurassic Period, these dinosaurs came to dominate the land, oceans and air. Dinosaurs in various shapes and sizes inhabited nearly the entire planet. Eventually, birds evolved during this period as well.

Sometime during the Cretaceous Period, around 65 million years ago, the dinosaurs somehow became extinct. There are many theories on how this occurred, but one thing is certain: Whatever wiped out the dinosaurs did not kill all the reptiles on Earth. In fact, not long after the extinction of the dinosaurs, other large reptiles continued to roam the planet. The giant Mosasaur was one of these survivors. It lived in the ocean and swam using its short paddles and long tail. In the air, Pterosaurs, a flying lizard, still survived.

The gecko of today is the evolutionary descendent of those reptiles that survived beyond the dinosaurs. Geckos have a lot in common with their prehistoric ancestors, and little has changed in their biology over the eons. In fact, geckos are among the most primitive lizards alive today. We can appreciate our pet geckos as not only links to nature, but links to the very distant past.

Humans and Geckos

No one knows exactly when human beings began keeping lizards as pets, but we can surmise that the practice started a long time ago. It is clear through both art and scientific literature that our species has been fascinated by lizards for thousands of years.

Geckos have lived in close association with humans for a long time. Geckos in various parts of the world can be found cohabitating with humans in their dwellings. These are not "pet" geckos per se, but rather wild lizards that have wandered into human homes in pursuit of insects. Because geckos are so good at eating bugs, they are welcome in most homes. In fact, in Malaysia having a tokay gecko in your home is considered good luck.

In the southwestern United States, geckos lived closely with Native Americans in the desert environment. These geckos, which were probably ancestors of the banded geckos we see today, were often the subject of Native American art. Their images have survived in the form of rock art, pottery, jewelry and fetishes. The stylized representation of a gecko shown on so much Native American art has even come to represent the spirit of the Southwest.

Human admiration for the gecko eventually culminated in North America in the late twentieth century. People in both the United States and Canada began developing a strong interest in keeping these fascinating lizards as pets. While in the 1960s and 1970s geckos were only rarely seen in pet stores, a small lizard called the anole was commonly sold as a pet. These hardy little lizards were sold as pets for children. There was also a trend in the 1950s for women to "wear" anoles on their clothing. The lizard would be attached to a pin with a small leash.

People have been charmed by geckos for many years; some, such as the tokay gecko, are considered good luck.

In the last decade there has been a huge increase in the popularity of lizards as pets (not as pins) with both children and adults. Consequently, there are now a number of lizard species available to the average reptile fan.

Because many gecko species are easy to breed in captivity and even easier to keep, the gecko in particular has grown in popularity. Nearly every pet store in the United States that sells lizards carries geckos. The leopard gecko is the most popular gecko pet and is readily available to any lizard keeper.

chapter 3

Eye
Lid
Geckos

All reptiles are organized into a scientific system that enables us to understand what they are and how they got there. To begin, leopard geckos are lizards. To get a little more specific, the scientific system breaks down lizards into groups called orders, and further breaks down orders into families. Geckos are their own family.

Geckos are a complicated group with many interesting twists and turns. This complexity makes them very exciting to study and keep. The level of diversity in this one branch of lizards is so complex and specialized it can inspire and dazzle.

The Leopard Gecko's
Scientific Classification

The chart on the following page shows how science classifies leopard geckos. The chart starts with the most basic part, class. The class *Reptilia* tells us that leopard geckos are reptiles. The order *Squamata* tells us they are in the group of snakes and lizards. The suborder *Sauria* tells us they are specialty lizards. The intermediate order *Gekkota* tells us they are in a group of lizards that includes geckos and pygpods (legless lizards). The family *Gekkonidae* is the geckos. The subfamily *Eublepharinae* is the whole group of primitive, specialized geckos with eye lids. The genus is where things get very specific. The genus *Eublepharis* narrows the gecko's characteristics down to very similar details that make a group of geckos closely related.

The Juvenile
Leopard Gecko

Each species has features that make it unique on a very detailed level. Some different species within a genus may look superficially similar, but have definite differences in scale counts, bone structure, lung structure or other not-so-obvious hidden differences that make them unique. These small differences may seem trivial, but can represent important changes taking place within a genus, or adaptations that evolved in isolated groups that can teach us about animals' abilities to adapt and change.

Class:	*Reptilia*	
Order:	*Squamata*	
Suborder:	*Sauria*	
Intermediate Order:	*Gekkota*	
Family:	*Gekkonidae*	
Subfamily:	*Eublepharinae*	
Genus:	*Eublepharis*	
Species:	*macularius*	

The Subfamily *Eublepharinae*

Leopard geckos belong to a special group of geckos, called the eye lid geckos. The name *Eublepharis* means "eye lid." These lizards are the most primitive geckos. All the members of this group have eyes with lids that can close. This feature is unique among geckos. In all

other groups of geckos the eye lids are fused open, and the geckos are unable to blink.

Leopard gecko eyes also have elongated slit-shaped, rather than round, pupils. Diurnal geckos, geckos that are active during daylight, have round pupils. If

you look closely at a gecko's eyes, you will notice the slit. The slit pupil opens widely in the dark to allow the maximum levels of light into the eye. This slit pupil enables the gecko to see better in limited light. Bright light will close the slit pupil.

Another Member of the Leopard Gecko Family

Another feature unique to this family of geckos is that they all lack the adhesive lamellae on their toes that enable other geckos to climb walls and glass. The *Eublepharis* geckos are predominantly terrestrial and do not climb well. They have adapted to life on the ground.

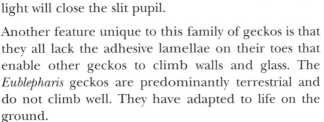

Leopard geckos belong to the genus *Eublepharis.* This genus has five species: *E. angramainyu, E. hardwicki, E. fuscus, E. turcmenicus* and *E. macularius.* These species all inhabit fairly dry areas. *Eublepharis macularius* is the leopard gecko. The word macularius means "spotted."

Only the leopard gecko, *E. macularius,* appears in the pet trade. *E. angramainyu* is one of the largest and is from Iran. *E. fuscus* may be the largest of the genus. This gecko lives in India. Published reports of this species of gecko reaching 10 inches, snout to vent length, exist. A 10-inch gecko would be a true giant of the genus.

Eublepharis
macula*ı* ius—
*the Leopard
Gecko*

CENTRAL AMERICAN GECKOS

The most commonly encountered gecko in the pet trade is *C. mitratus* from Central America, commonly called the Central American banded gecko. Dealers often import this species for the pet trade, and breeders commonly breed it in captivity. While generally easy to care for, this gecko has a more skittish personality than a leopard gecko. It is often secretive and runs into a hiding area as soon as someone approaches it. It can also bite in self-defense. Despite its cautious behavior, it is beautiful and fascinating to watch in a terrarium.

Central American geckos breed well in captivity and can vary greatly in pattern. This variety makes them ideal for breeders, as these geckos can be bred for outstanding colors and unique patterns. Breeders currently breed them in several pattern forms. By selectively breeding geckos with similar patterns, breeders bring out some attractive characteristics.

The reticulated form is a light pattern with small broken patches of darker tan on an ochre background. Rather than bold banding, this phase features a subtle, even pattern. Breeders have also established a jungle phase. Jungle phases are named after their resemblance to a camouflage pattern. This pattern is extremely attractive with large swirling bands of black.

FAT TAILED GECKOS

The fat tailed geckos (*Hemitheconyx caudicinctus*) of West Africa are also members of the eye lid gecko family. These geckos are common in the pet trade. They can have dispositions similar to those of leopard geckos. Many breeders produce this species in several pattern phases. The banded pattern, featuring dark brown on light brown in bands crossing the body, is the most common. The striped pattern, the most in demand, is striking. The striped phase is a white stripe running from the top of the gecko's head to the tip of its tail. The

white stripe varies in thickness. Breeders are now producing an amelanistic phase. The amelanistic gecko is a gecko whose skin lacks melanin, which creates the dark pigmentation. Like an albino, this gecko is extremely light in color. Unlike a true albino, this gecko has regular, dark-colored eyes. The general skin tone is a cream color with the pattern subtly visible in lighter shades. These specimens are reportedly very sensitive to bright light.

These two geckos demonstrate the difference between the leopard gecko (top) and the fat tailed gecko (below).

21

THE GENUS *GONIUROSAURUS*

Common names for the geckos of the *Goniurosaurus* genus are Japanese cave geckos, Chinese cave geckos or Chinese leopard geckos. These eye lid geckos are somewhat fragile and require very specific care. They are secretive and seldom seen in the pet trade. This group is very exciting, as new species have recently been discovered in Vietnam and two species, yet to be described and given scientific names, have become fairly easy to

*A Baby Albino
Leopard Gecko*

acquire in the pet trade because they breed readily and thrive in captivity. The common names for these two species are the yellow banded and purple banded cave geckos. They were imported into the United States in 1996 as *Goniurosaurus lichtenfelderi* and *G. l. hainenensis*. Scientists have discovered that these identifications are incorrect and that each gecko is a new species. The geckos are currently being described and soon we will have names to call them!

*The Japanese
Leopard Gecko:*
Goniurosaurus
Kroiwae
splendens

A group of this genus of geckos inhabits various islands of Japan. These geckos are not very well known in captivity and have only recently been studied. They are the Japanese cave geckos (*Goniurosaurus kuroiwae*). There are five subspecies of this gecko. The subspecies include *G. k. kuroiwae, G. k. orientalis, G. k. splendens, G.k. toyamai,* and *G. k. yamashinae.* Laws protect most subspecies of this group throughout their range and you will not find them in the hobby.

THE GENUS *HOLODACTYLUS*

Two very attractive (and very difficult to keep) members of the eye lid gecko group is the Tanzanian African clawed gecko (*Holodactylus africanus*) and the very rare, larger *Holodactylus cornii* from Somolia. The clawed gecko has a very small, flat tail and looks slightly like a smaller version of the fat tailed gecko. It spends most of its time underground in damp burrows. One of the keys to keeping this gecko healthy is having a damp area of substrate in its environment.

*The Chinese
Leopard Gecko*

Breeders seldom breed the clawed gecko in captivity. Imported clawed geckos frequently arrive in very dehydrated conditions from which they rarely recover. Importers often avoid bringing them for this reason. Even when they do thrive, they spend most of their time underground where no one sees them.

THE CAT GECKO

The rarest eye lid gecko is the cat gecko (*Aeluroscalabotes felinis* and the subspecies *A.f. multituberculatus*). The cat gecko is a secretive gecko from the rain forests of Malaysia, Thailand and Borneo. It is the most primitive member of the gecko family and has several substantial differences from the other members.

Unlike all other *Eublepharis* geckos, this species is arboreal. It is well adapted to climbing, while still lacking the adhesive lamellae that all other arboreal geckos have. Instead, it has specialized opposable toes and a prehensile tail that enable it to climb with ease. The tail often acts as a fifth limb in securing a foothold when climbing. Like a leopard gecko, the cat gecko is slow and deliberate in its movements, and it tends to have a gentle disposition.

Some say the tail of a cat gecko resembles a toxic caterpillar. When disturbed, a cat gecko sometimes raises its tail high and partially curls it, perhaps hoping its predator will think this meal should be avoided. The

The Cat Gecko:
Aeluroscala-
botes felinis

regrown tail of a cat gecko resembles a caterpillar even more than the original.

While they are rarely seen in the wild, cat geckos are even rarer in captivity. They spend their days hidden away, curled up in a humid area. When they are available in the hobby, they are usually wild-caught geckos. So far, only a couple of breeders have produced them. Repeated breeding has been difficult. Their captive care requires exacting temperatures and humidity levels. Due to their demanding care these geckos are best left to very serious, experienced hobbyists.

chapter 4

Why a Leopard Gecko?

Lizards as Pets

There is generally a great interest in keeping lizards as pets. Smaller lizards like leopard geckos have several advantages that make them ideal to keep in the home. Unlike cats or dogs, leopard geckos have minimal care requirements. They can be left for a cou-

ple of days without the need for someone to come in and take care of them. Lights can be put on timers, and food items and water can be left in feeding dishes to supply all their needs while you are away. They do not need attention or affection to thrive. They are quiet. They do not smell. They also do not affect people with dog or cat allergies.

While many lizards can be tricky to keep and some grow very large, it is not the case with the leopard gecko. They grow to an approximate length of 10 inches. This size allows for caging that fits restricted space in small apartments, in an office or in a young person's bedroom.

In addition to being beautiful, the leopard gecko is a perfect low-maintenance pet.

IGUANAS

Iguanas are popular in pet stores, but they need a very specialized diet and grow to $5\frac{1}{2}$ feet in length. They also require special lighting to stay healthy. Very few people have the room and time for such a demanding animal.

TOKAY GECKOS

Another lizard that pet stores commonly sell is the tokay gecko (*Gekko gecko*). They are large geckos reaching 12 inches in length and have a bite to match. In addition to being more than willing to bite, they do not release their grip easily. Even cage cleaning can be tricky, as tokay geckos are very fast and can climb walls easily. You are better off leaving these geckos to very experienced hobbyists.

ANOLES

Anoles (*Anolis carolinis*) are another type of lizard that virtually every pet shop sells. They are very inexpensive, and people frequently purchase them as first pet lizards. Dealers often present them as American chameleons, but they are not true chameleons; they get their common name from their ability to change from green to brown.

A desire to match a background and blend into it does not influence the color change; the lizard's mood and need to adjust its body temperature directly causes the change. When they are scared, upset or angry they will darken and turn brown. When they are cold and have access to sunlight or a basking light, they will darken as well, to better absorb the heat and warm up.

These small, quick lizards are not very good pets for most people. Their diet requires very small insects, which makes it difficult for most people to feed them. They also need special lighting and do not like to be touched or held. Even cleaning their cage requires delicate movements because they can dart out of the smallest opening and escape.

The Perfect Lizard Pet

Leopard geckos are as close to a perfect lizard pet as you can get. Besides the fact that they are attractive and easy to care for, they are the most widely captive-produced geckos in the world. Breeders breed thousands every year to supply the pet trade. This captive production is important for several reasons, one being that they are not taken from the wild. Wild-caught geckos present a whole range of problems, from environmental concerns to issues about the geckos' health.

AVAILABILITY

Another reason leopard geckos are nearly perfect is their availability for the average person. Nearly every pet store in the United States sells them. Reptile expos, held year-round in many cities, always have several breeders of leopard geckos in attendance. Reptile magazines advertise many breeders, often with photos depicting stunning specimens. Even surfing the Internet will yield many choices for buying or trading leopard geckos.

EASY HANDLING

Physically leopard geckos are impressive animals. They are the perfect size for a pet lizard. A typical adult averages 8 inches in length, which is a very manageable size. The body is fairly heavy and thick, giving it a sturdy feel. This size allows for comfortable handling. Small children can hold a leopard gecko without the gecko intimidating them. The leopard gecko's space requirements are minimal and even small apartments can accommodate them. The caging need not be enormous for these geckos to thrive. A common 10-gallon fish tank often serves as an ideal-sized home for a single leopard gecko. The habits of the leopard gecko make tasks such as cage cleaning quick and easy. (Cage maintenance will be covered in later chapters.)

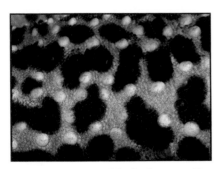

The Skin Pattern of the Adult Leopard Gecko

VARIETY

Leopard geckos are extremely attractive animals. The average leopard gecko is yellow with many black spots, hence its name. The color patterns are extremely variable. This variability has allowed skilled breeders to create beautiful versions of the standard yellow with dark spots. Breeders have achieved some stunning results by doing some selective breeding of geckos with similar patterns.

Color, Pattern and Phase

When discussing leopard geckos the following three terms are commonly used: color, pattern and phase.

Color is the color of the base of the lizard's skin.

Patterns are the designs created by the arrangement of the gecko's black spots.

Phase is another term to describe the particular attributes of a breeder's geckos.

Always keep in mind marketing techniques when hearing of a new phase of designer leopard gecko. When sales may be slow, some business-oriented breeders may release a new phase name, intending to increase interest in and sales of their product. Use your judgement when evaluating a new phase. Sometimes it can be a stretch of the imagination, and other times it will be truly new and stunning. Surprises always crop up now and then, like the new albino leopard geckos. When choosing a designer gecko, always base your decision on your real feelings. If you like the way the gecko looks, and appreciate its beauty, then you have found the gecko that is for you.

chapter 5

Patterns, Colors and Phases

of

Leopard Geckos

This chapter covers the various patterns, colors and phases that you may encounter in your search for a leopard gecko.

High Yellow—This gecko has fewer spots than other leopard geckos on a bright-yellow body. This phase can vary greatly between breeders. Some geckos will have fewer spots than others. High yellow has generally become the standard leopard gecko. The fewer the spots, the higher the cost of the gecko.

Albino or Amelanistic—An albino gecko is cream color with pink eyes. Breeders have been hoping to attain this mutation for years, and recently several breeders have succeeded in producing albinos at generally the same time. Because there is usually a large interest

30

among hobbyists in owning albino forms of reptiles, breeders expect that it will hold true for the large-scale production of albino leopard geckos. The addition of this form will change the number of available phases in amazing ways over the next few years. Within a fairly short time you can expect to see albino stripes and eventually albino snow leopard (see the explanation of the snow pattern, below) geckos, which would be patternless and pure white in color.

Albino Patternless or Amelanistic Patternless—An albino patternless gecko is a cream-colored gecko with no trace of the spotting or banding of a regular albino. This phase was created by line breeding a patternless gecko to an albino.

Leusistic—True leusistic geckos are pure white with dark eyes. One breeder noticed this mutation and has started a breeding program. Due to leopard geckos' fast maturation and prolific nature they should be available within a short time. The first offerings will be very expensive, but within one year prices will drop considerably.

The Leusistic Leopard Gecko

Patternless—Patternless geckos have an even yellow background color and no spotting or banding. When these geckos are born, they are spotted and have dark pigmentation, but as they grow older they lose all patterns and are an even yellow color. Some are darker yellow; these geckos are in less demand. Dealers

31

mistakenly applied the term "leusistic" to these geckos when they first became available, but people continue to use the term. As word gets out that these lizards are truly a patternless phase people will stop using the term "leusistic."

Snow—These geckos have the normal color patterns, except they will be on a white background instead of yellow.

Striped—This attractive gecko has a lightly colored stripe running from the top of its head down the back to the tip of its tail. Thin black stripes outline this light stripe on both sides. A striped gecko can be difficult to find, as producing stripes can be tricky.

Reverse Stripe—The reverse stripe phase is the opposite of the striped phase: White stripes outline a dark stripe on either side, down the gecko's back to the tip of its tail.

Jungle—These geckos have black spots that connect in random patterns reminiscent of camouflage patterns, but using only yellow and black. The best examples of this phase have large areas of bright yellow with very unusual, irregular patterns made up of black. Jungle phase leopard geckos have a great deal of variability. Breeders who look very closely and hold back unusual specimens for breeding can produce many unique designs. The jungle phase may be the best for unusual designs, due to the connect-the-dots nature of the patterning. No two jungle phase leopard geckos look alike.

Circle Back—This gecko has a black circle, made up of connected spots, similar to a bull's-eye on its back. Julie Bergman, owner of the Gecko Ranch in Northern California, noticed a nearly complete circle of connected dots during her gecko-breeding efforts and worked to eventually produce animals with a full circle.

Lavender Leopard—Leopard geckos tend to have a lavender tint in the white areas of their skin. Many generations of selective breeding have produced geckos with large and brighter areas of lavender.

Tangerine—These geckos have large areas of bright orange colors. The more orange pigmentation in the gecko, the more expensive it is to purchase. A breeder developed this phase after noticing a small area of orange on the rear legs of some specimens. Retaining these color areas and watching the outcome of breedings have led to increased orange pigmentation with each generation. These geckos have generated a great deal of excitement among keepers, and they are in high demand.

No matter what variety your gecko is, it will make an interesting and educational pet.

Melanistic—A melanistic gecko is an almost completely black or very dark gecko with little or no pattern showing. After years of developing brighter and

33

lighter geckos, some breeders realized they could develop an all-black gecko by retaining darker animals over successive generations. Naturally many wild-caught leopard geckos are very much darker than their commercially bred counterparts. Even the plainest of commonly bred geckos are brighter than many wild geckos. A few breeders have selected the darkest of these animals to breed. As yet unnamed, perhaps breeders will call them Black Panthers.

chapter 6

Your Leopard Gecko's Behavior

With Audrey Pavia

One of the best things about owning a gecko is observing its behavior. Geckos are interesting creatures and can provide you with hours of observational enjoyment.

Hunting

Geckos are excellent hunters and are entertaining to watch.

Pay attention to your gecko the next time you feed it. Geckos are opportunistic feeders and won't deliberately go searching for prey. But if an unsuspecting insect comes within their field of vision, watch out! Geckos rarely miss their prey.

If your gecko is feeling hungry and it spies an insect, it will begin to stalk the insect much like a cat would stalk a mouse. It will move with

Welcome to the World of the Leopard Gecko

a very deliberate and stilted motion, all the while focusing intently on its victim. Once it gets within striking distance, the gecko will take a second to get the insect directly "within its crosshairs," and then, in the blink of an eye, the insect will be inside the gecko's mouth. Sometimes, just before the gecko strikes, its tail begins to quiver intensely.

The next step in the process is to swallow the insect, which the gecko does with merely a few movements of its head. Many geckos will then lick their lips almost as if to say "Wow, that was good."

Crickets are a nutritious meal and make good prey for a hungry gecko. (Uroplatus sikorae)

Shedding

Another one of the gecko's interesting behaviors comes when it's time for the lizard to shed its skin. Just prior to molting, many geckos become less active. Then, as the skin begins to separate from the lizard's body, the gecko will try to help it along by pulling at it and swallowing it whole. Geckos can often be seen trying to pull the most stubborn pieces off their toes, much like a dog would try to chew a burr out of its fur.

Territoriality

Geckos, particularly males, are notorious for being territorial. In fact, male geckos will fight violently to protect their turf. The gecko prefaces an attack by threatening his foe with a bobbing of his head.

The main motivation behind this territoriality lies in the gecko's mating instinct. By protecting his territory, a male gecko is also protecting his right to breed with any females that are within the area. In captivity, male geckos will fight whether or not a female is present— the instinct is still there.

Female geckos occasionally become territorial as well, driven by an instinct to protect their nests and have access to the greatest food supply.

Mating

Most novice gecko owners are not ready to take on the hobby of breeding their geckos, since this can be a time-consuming and complicated task. However, it is interesting to note some of the different behavioral patterns that relate to gecko courtship.

When male and female geckos are introduced, the male will usually vocalize to her, making whatever sounds are inherent to his species. A circling ritual will also ensue, along with some head bobbing and tail writhing. This is the way male and female geckos "get acquainted," and a mating usually results soon after. Scientists also believe that this courtship might be instrumental in inducing ovulation in the female gecko.

SOME GECKOS ARE CLONES

Oddly enough, some gecko species are parthenogenetic, which means that the females can reproduce without a male partner. In these situations, the resulting offspring are actually genetic clones of the female. It is surmised that nature created this condition in order to help the species survive during times when the gecko population is low and mates are few and far between.

Nesting

Female geckos are not devout mothers like female mammals are, but they are more nurturing than many other reptiles. When a female is close to egg-laying time, she will select a secure place to deposit the eggs. The arboreal species tend to glue their eggs high up so they hang vertically. Terrestrial species lay their eggs on the ground, usually in a secure spot rich in substrate.

The females of some gecko species will actually protect their eggs, fighting with other geckos that get too close to the nest. In fact, both the male and female tokay gecko will guard the eggs and show aggression to any other lizard that nears the nest. Female tokay geckos have been known to cannibalize the eggs of other females, which explains this defensive behavior.

Terrestrial geckos usually lay their eggs in a safe area on the ground. This leopard gecko is emerging from its egg.

Hiding

Although hiding isn't exactly one of the most fascinating gecko behaviors to watch, it is nonetheless an important activity for the gecko. Nature has equipped geckos with the instinct to take cover when they are sleeping so predators won't make a meal out of them when they are most vulnerable.

Different species of geckos prefer to hide in different ways. Arboreal species, like the tokay gecko, prefer to tuck their bodies behind leaves and under peeling bark. Some terrestrial species, like the thick tailed gecko, prefer to hide on the ground under leaf litter. Other terrestrial geckos, like the leopard gecko, are happy to stash their bodies away beneath a piece of wood or rock.

Hiding is such an important behavior in geckos that any gecko which isn't provided a hiding place can become so stressed it will get sick and die.

The Gecko Personality

Although geckos don't have the same kind of behavioral traits as mammals, they do nonetheless have distinctive personalities. Indeed, different species are inclined toward different kinds of temperaments. While leopard geckos tend to be quiet and easy-going, tokays are aggressive and hard to handle. Banded geckos prefer to hide all day under a rock or piece of wood, while day geckos want to be out in the sunshine, watching the world go by.

By taking the time to quietly watch your gecko, you'll discover its unique personality.

Gecko personalities are not only unique to their species, but also to each individual lizard. Anyone who has spent any quality time around geckos will agree with this observation.

Geckos are fascinating to watch, not only because they are beautiful, but also because they have real personality. The best way to discover your particular gecko's distinct personality is to quietly observe it. Keep its terrarium in a place that is relatively peaceful yet where you spend enough time so as to notice its activities.

If you watch your pet closely, you'll discover all kinds of things about its personality. You will probably see that it has certain preferences when it comes to food. Your gecko may look nonchalantly at crickets and only hunt them when it's really hungry, but pounce on mealworms the instant you place them in its enclosure.

You may also notice that your particular gecko likes to perch in a certain spot in its terrarium, looking down over its enclosure like a king observing its domain. Or, it could be the type that prefers to lie around underneath its hiding place or an overhanging leaf rather than take in the big picture.

If you have more than one gecko of the same species, you will clearly see differences in each individual. Every gecko is a unique being, with its own special preferences and characteristics. One of the most interesting and fun aspects of gecko ownership is discovering the particular nuances of your individual pet.

The Outside World

You may think your gecko's world is limited only to what is going on inside its terrarium, but this is not true. I discovered this firsthand one day shortly after acquiring Gordon, my leopard gecko. I had placed a white container of crickets on the floor near Gordon's terrarium, which is in my home office (a great place to keep your gecko's enclosure, by the way). As I sat at my computer working, I noticed that Gordon had come out of his hiding place and was standing with his nose up against the glass, staring intently in the direction of the cricket container. I glanced over at the container, wondering what he was looking at, and discovered that an army of tiny black ants had attacked my crickets! Thanks to Gordon's acute observation, I was able to rescue my crickets from a league of marauding ants.

You may not have had the chance to experience anything quite like this scene, but if you pay close attention, you'll notice that *your* gecko is aware of its outside surroundings, too. If you ever have to move your pet's enclosure, you'll see plenty of evidence of your pet's observational abilities.

When you move your gecko's enclosure from one place to another, you will probably notice a significant increase in your pet's activity. If you have a nocturnal gecko that usually hides during the day, you'll see your pet come out of its hiding place and start exploring the edges of its terrarium with avid curiosity, looking out through the glass in an obvious attempt to figure out what's going on. It's also possible that your nocturnal gecko may become frightened by what is happening and will quickly sequester itself in its hiding place, refusing to come out until things have settled down.

If you have a diurnal gecko, it will also take note of the change in scenery. You'll see it looking around, noticing that its enclosure no longer has the same outside scenery as it did before. If it gets nervous, it may find itself a cozy leaf to hide under.

A nocturnal gecko, such as the popular leopard gecko, may respond to a change in its surroundings by spending more time than usual out and about in the daylight.

Even though the interior of its terrarium has stayed the same, this change in the outside world can be rather stressful for your pet. To help it adjust to its new surroundings, avoid handling it for several days before and after the move. You should also withhold food during that time because stress is particularly taxing for geckos with full stomachs. Let your gecko settle in before you offer it food in its new home.

Note: Before you pick up your gecko's terrarium and move it elsewhere, remove the water dish and any other accessories that could injure your pet should they topple over and fall on him during the jostling that always occurs during a move.

Another example of your gecko's awareness to the outside world is how it reacts to other pets you may have.

If you have a cat or dog, and your pet likes to sit out-side your gecko's enclosure and watch it, your gecko will surely notice. If the dog or cat sits quietly and is not threatening (and you have a particularly mellow gecko species), this can be an acceptable arrangement. However, if your cat or dog runs around, jumps on top of the terrarium or, worse yet, tries to break into it, your gecko will be stressed by what is going on outside its home. Keep your cat or dog away from your gecko's terrarium if the animal does anything other than sit quietly and observe.

As you can see, your gecko is very sensitive to changes in its environment. For this reason, it's best to leave the accessories and dishes inside the terrarium in the same place. Geckos are creatures of habit and expect to find their hiding places, water dishes, and other cage acces-sories in the same place every day. "Redecorating" just for the sake of change may be fun for you, but it will be very stressful for your gecko!

Change of Seasons

Just about every creature on the planet notices when the seasons start to change. The seasons are part of the cycle of life, and even tiny insects are sensitive to them.

Your gecko is no exception to this rule. Geckos re-spond to the changes in temperature and light when in the wild, so it's only natural they should notice these things in captivity, too. In fact, people who breed geckos will create artificial winter and summer using con-trolled lighting to encourage their animals to breed.

Nocturnal geckos that have no source of artificial light in their terrariums are most likely to take notice when the sun begins to noticeably set earlier in the day dur-ing the fall or later in the day during the spring. Even though the pets are indoors and are provided with an artificial heat source, they also tend to be aware of the change in temperature from warm seasons to cool, and vice versa.

You can tell that your pet is responding to the change in seasons by observing its activity. Geckos tend to be more active in the warmer seasons than the cooler ones, so you may notice a difference in your pet when summer's heat turns to autumn cool. It may begin to eat a little bit less and spend less time moving around its enclosure. Although geckos don't hibernate, they do have a reduction in activity during the cooler months. Make sure you compensate for this change in weather by providing an adequate heat source for your pet.

You may also notice a behavior change in your gecko when winter turns to spring. Your lazy lizard may start coming out from its hiding space more often and be a little more interested in those crickets and mealworms now that the sun is staying in the sky a bit longer. Enjoy your pet's subtle reactions to the seasons while still providing it with the natural heat source it requires to stay healthy. Let it help you celebrate the changing seasons in its own, lizardlike fashion.

Home Alone

Because we humans are such social creatures, it can be hard for us to understand animals that do not need the interaction of their own kind. In the wild, geckos are solitary creatures that establish their own territory where they live, hunt and breed. Male geckos will fight vehemently to defend this territory from other male geckos, and, in fact, some will not tolerate the presence of other geckos at all except during breeding time.

> **BE AWARE OF SALMONELLA**
>
> All victims of a salmonella outbreak in Denver, Colorado, had a few things in common that pointed to reptiles as the source of the infection. They all had visited the Denver Zoo, all had eaten finger food there (hot dogs, hamburgers or sandwiches) and all had touched or pressed up against the railing of the Komodo Dragon Lizard (*Varanus komodiensis*) exhibit. The same serotype of salmonella with which these victims were infected was cultured off the railing. This finding proved that even surfaces touched by a reptile can be responsible for salmonella infection.

You may feel a bit uncomfortable with the idea of keeping your gecko all by itself in a terrarium because you may have the notion that the gecko is lonely. If your gecko had the psyche of a human being—or even a dog or cat—your notion would be correct. Most mammals thrive on the companionship of others, especially our domesticated friends.

Your gecko is a whole different critter, however. By providing it with a space that it can call its own, without other geckos to compete with for food or space, you are actually doing it a favor! Geckos prefer to be alone most of the time. It is less stressful for them, and because stress can be damaging to a gecko's immune system, it is ultimately the healthiest way to keep them.

A Different Kind of Animal

Your gecko is nothing like a human or even a dog or a cat when it comes to behavior. But that's okay. It is this uniqueness that makes the gecko so special in our world.

Learn to appreciate your gecko's special ways by learning as much as you can about it and observing its behavior at every opportunity. Soon you will come to realize that geckos are quite wonderous creatures that should be appreciated for the unique critters that they are.

Geckos are more fun to handle than other lizards because they have a tendency to trust humans.

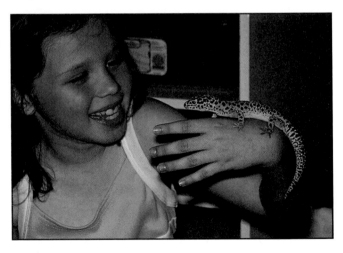

Handling a Leopard Gecko

Perhaps the most endearing quality of geckos is their behavior when handled. Unlike many other species of lizard, these lizards are very trusting. They can sit in your hand and be content, or they may slowly explore.

They make slow, deliberate movements and are not prone to quick bursts of speed. Climbing up your arm and onto your shoulder is a common occurrence. Be sure to sit very still, so your gecko doesn't fall. You may want to wear a long-sleeved shirt as a gecko walking up your arm will tickle and may cause your arm to be unsteady.

Always remember to wash well after you handle your gecko. One cannot overemphasize the importance of this washing. While geckos are not generally dirty, they are animals. They may have walked through feces and have residue on their tails, or they may have defecated in a water dish and then walked through the dish. Such an occurrence can leave bacteria on their skin that can make you ill. It is not necessary to fear this bacteria and avoid handling your gecko, but you do need to wash after handling to be on the safe side. Commercial antibacterial soaps work very well for cleanup. Get in the habit of washing after handling and cage cleaning.

Leopard geckos are not prone to biting and do not bite when handled carefully. While a bite is not probable, always handle leopard geckos with gentle care and respect. You may not realize your movements are rough or too fast. Never grab a gecko's tail or grab a gecko behind its head. Doing so will scare it and may induce it to bite.

The Leopard Gecko's Tail

Take extra care not to handle your gecko's tail. The tail will easily snap off if a gecko is picked up by the tail, or grabbed by the tail. Get in the habit of not touching your gecko's tail.

6
Your Leopard
Gecko's
Behavior

Be sure to handle your leopard gecko with care.

Captive-Bred vs. Wild-Caught Leopard Geckos

Breeders readily produce leopard geckos in captivity. This fact is very important for several reasons. In buying a captive-bred gecko you can rest assured that you have not contributed to the capture and removal of animals from their natural habitat. The wild areas of the world are shrinking, and many populations of wild-animal life are at risk. Mass collection for the pet trade can certainly have an impact on wild populations.

If you are careful with your gecko, it should not bite you.

Gecko health is also at risk when buying wild-caught animals. Geckos can sustain injuries from the collection process or from the hazards of living in the wild. Many wild-caught geckos will have scar tissue from healed injuries and regrown tails. Wild-caught geckos

require special care in acclimating to captivity. They will be less inclined to act as calm as captive-bred geckos.

One very serious health issue is internal parasites. Wild-caught geckos frequently have internal parasites that require a veterinarian's care to remove. There are many types of roundworms, hookworms and protozoan and flagellate parasites that are common in the wild. A wild-caught gecko will require a fecal exam for a veterinarian to determine if and what type of parasites may exist and to prescribe appropriate medications.

It is a good idea to have an annual fecal exam on your animal as a precaution. The exam, performed at a veterinarian's office, is usually inexpensive. It is well worth the trip. When getting a fecal exam, bring a fresh stool sample in a plastic bag. Collect the sample and bring it to the vet as soon as possible. The vet will look for living parasites, so do not freeze the sample.

Treatment is often easy and successful. The proper treatment does, however, require a veterinarian's care. Treatment and office visits can be expensive. For this reason alone, buying a captive-bred animal is often an exceptional bargain.

Many breeders with booths at herp shows are great resources for quality geckos.

Despite the drawbacks, one should not completely frown upon the act of importing wild-caught specimens. These specimens are of great importance in starting captive populations, and in adding genetic diversity to limited captive gene pools. However, these geckos should not be part of the retail pet trade. Unsuspecting buyers who purchase these animals unaware of the added care they require may be sadly disappointed when their animal does not thrive. Some uncaring retailers have been known to sell wild-caught geckos as captive bred, so be careful when selecting a retailer. When making a selection, it is always a good idea to ask if the gecko is captive bred.

Is This Gecko Wild Caught or Captive Bred?

There are several things to look for when trying to evaluate a gecko you suspect may be wild caught. Always be wary when you see a full-grown adult gecko for sale. Breeders sell most captive-bred geckos as either juveniles or young adults because it is expensive to raise a gecko to adult size for resale. Most buyers are not willing to pay the substantial extra cost for an adult captive-bred gecko. Remember, it takes almost a year for a gecko to reach a mature size. During this time a breeder must feed and house these animals, and adult geckos require a great deal of space.

When first evaluating a gecko, look closely at the tail. If you see a regrown tail, you should be cautious. Regrown tails are easy to recognize: The texture is smoother than the texture of an original tail and the scales are smaller, giving the tail a very even look. A regrown tail also lacks the ringed annulation. This ringed texture gives the tail its unique look. The regrown tail will also be shorter and fatter.

Wild-caught leopard geckos also tend to look generally darker and less colorful than most captive-bred geckos. They tend to have more spotting and duller yellows. They are also generally not as calm as captive-bred geckos.

The cost difference between captive-bred and wild-caught geckos is very minimal. In many cases captive-bred animals cost about twice as much as the wild-caught version, but it should not be the case with leopard geckos. Breeders have become very adept at providing quality animals at reasonable costs. Leopard geckos have become one of the most affordable reptile pets available, although specialty designer geckos will cost substantially more due to the painstaking, careful selective breeding necessary to produce these beauties.

> ## A DELICATE BALANCE
>
> Every natural habitat develops so as to provide for all of its residents. For example, in a given environment, insects serve as food for reptiles and amphibians that in turn serve as food for birds. When a species is eliminated from the environment, or a species is introduced by humans, the natural balance of the habitat is disrupted. To do your part in maintaining the balance, leave wild animals in the wild, and do not release pet species into a wild environment.

The Natural Habitat of the Leopard Gecko

The natural range of leopard geckos is Eastern Afghanistan, Pakistan and Northwestern India. This region consists of rocky desert and savanna. The area is generally semiarid, but leopard geckos also inhabit areas with moisture. The terrain ranges from sandy gravel to hard clay soil with a sandy covering. Vegetation consists of bushes and grasses.

Leopard geckos prefer to be under rocks and in holes underground. They remain hidden during the day, and become active at dusk. This region gets cold during the winter months, and these geckos take refuge underground from mid-December to mid- to late

February. In the Peshawar area of Pakistan the temperatures can get to a low of 41° F (5° C) at night and 59° F (15° C) during the day in January. In the summer things can become quite hot. During the peak of summer temperatures can reach 104° F (40° C) during the day and 77° F (25° C) at night.

In the wild leopard geckos can have many enemies. Nocturnal hunters like foxes, snakes and birds of prey all can and do exploit leopard geckos. Long periods of drought, heavy rains and people encroaching into leopard gecko habitat all play a role in restricting this gecko's ability to survive in the wild. The life span of a leopard gecko in the wild is unknown, but certainly shorter than life in captivity.

This gecko enclosure approximates the natural habitat of the gecko, which is usually rocky and sandy.

Caring

for Your

part two

Leopard Gecko

chapter 7

Selecting
Your
Leopard
Gecko

Once you have decided the leopard gecko is for you, you will need to find one.

Selecting the right leopard gecko is important, so take your time and choose carefully. Review all the colors and patterns ahead of time. Know the animal. Always plan ahead and have a terrarium set up in advance. Have food insects available as well.

Where to Look

Places for selecting your leopard gecko range from your local pet store, local breeders and reptile expos to mail order from specialized breeders.

LOCAL HERPETOLOGICAL
SOCIETY MEETINGS

Local herpetological society meetings are great places
to find leopard geckos and a support network. Nearly
every state has a herpetological society.

If you live in the vicinity of a herp society, you should
attend meetings and will most likely find members who
breed geckos and bring them to meetings for sale to
other members. At these meetings you will find a
friendly atmosphere with many knowledgeable society
members ready to offer you information and moral
support.

PET STORES

Pet stores may be the easiest starting point for most
people. Nearly every town has one, and the shopkeep-
ers can order what you want, if they do not have it in
stock. The drawback is that unless you know and trust
your local retailer, you have no idea
where your leopard gecko came
from or if it is healthy.

Many pet stores order every reptile
from a wholesaler. These animals
may be wild caught, or dealers may
have caged them with wild-caught
animals. This possibility is a very
important concern. Even if the animal is captive bred, if anyone caged
it with wild-caught animals, it may
have been exposed to disease and
parasites.

Also, because they have space limi-
tations and the animals are usually
in the store for a short period, pet stores sometimes
cage multiple species within the same display cage.
One day a wild-caught gecko may be in a display cage,
and then the next day a leopard gecko is placed in the
same cage. Busy pet stores don't always have the time
to sterilize a cage between animals. Sterilizing the cage
prevents transmission of diseases and parasites.

> **JOIN YOUR LOCAL
> HERPETOLOGICAL
> SOCIETY**
>
> Enhance the educational value of
> your pet lizard by joining a local
> herpetological society. These
> groups will conduct seminars and
> provide literature on all aspects of
> lizard care. Other experienced
> lizard owners can share their tips
> with you. Best of all, many soci-
> eties work to ensure the safety of
> lizards in their natural environ-
> ment. By getting involved, you can
> learn about lizards and help to
> protect them at the same time.

53

The selection of animals in a pet store will also be limited, as only one or two geckos may be available at a time. Being able to see a few different color phases may be important to a prospective buyer.

Make sure that the retailer knows proper care of this species and will be able to assist you in your questions. Ask if the retailer has experience with the species or can put you in contact with the breeder from which the retailer buys his or her geckos. If you hear statements you know are not true, take your business elsewhere.

Reptile shows are wonderful places to find your pet gecko.

REPTILE EXPOS

If you want the absolute largest number of animals from which to choose, attend a reptile expo. At an expo you can see all the different color phases and ranges in gecko age, and find the most competitive prices. Expos have become very common and are within driving distance of most major cities. Organizers hold them most frequently in late spring and early fall. In the late spring and fall you will find the largest available number of geckos, because in cooler months most breeders hibernate their geckos.

Choosing a breeder can be as important as choosing the gecko. Look at the overall presentation of the breeders' animals and access breeders' willingness to talk about the animals and their care.

**ATTEND A
HERP SHOW**

Herp expositions, where breeders display their wares, are frequently held all over the country. To locate a herp show, where you're bound to find lots of geckos for sale, check the listings in reptile-related magazines.

Most expos invite local herpetological societies. You can ask herp society volunteers to assist you in selecting an animal. Make sure the vendor from which you decide to purchase an animal is willing to answer all your questions, can provide a history of the animals and will be available after the sale. Finding a vendor willing to be available for questions is extremely important. Don't be afraid to ask questions.

The Ideal Age

When selecting a gecko, always ask how old the animal is. Do not purchase a very young hatchling; a gecko should be at least 6 weeks old when sold. At this age the gecko will be able to handle the change of environment.

When you bring an animal home and change its cage, it will go through a natural period of adjustment. During this period it may not eat and may remain hidden, which is normal. Usually within a couple days it will relax and begin to adjust. When a hatchling is sold too young, it does not have any fat reserves, and a period of not eating can be very detrimental.

These geckos are different ages. The largest is an adult, the medium-sized is 4 months old and the smallest is still a baby.

Sometimes breeders ship these animals to a wholesaler, who then ships them to a retailer. The process of shipping from breeder to wholesaler to retailer can be a fairly long period to go without food or water, especially for a hatchling. Some wholesalers may even cool down their stock so they do not have to feed or clean up after them.

If you want to breed geckos, avoid full adults. Sometimes breeders will sell off old stock that can no longer produce eggs. These animals can make good pets, but without knowing their age, you will not know how long they have to live. If you intend to breed your geckos and you buy an older animal, you may end up disappointed when it does not produce eggs.

It is best to buy a juvenile leopard gecko. They have adjusted to life. They are eating well, and they have some size on them. At this stage they will still have their juvenile color patterns as well.

Buying a leopard gecko at a young age is not essential, but it makes the process of raising a gecko fun. Watching them grow and change is one of the best parts of keeping this species. Raising a younger animal will also give you and the gecko a chance to get to know each other.

When You've Chosen Your Leopard Gecko

When you have selected a gecko, be prepared to ask the breeder or dealer some important questions. Ask what he or she is feeding his or her geckos. Some breeders use a specific food item, and your gecko may be used to that item. If you can have that type of insect ready, the period of acclimating can be easier.

KEY FACTORS IN CHOOSING A LIZARD

- How much space are you willing to devote to your lizard's cage?

- If you will have more than one lizard, do you have room to house them separately, if necessary?

- Will you be willing to feed your lizard insects?

- Will your children and other family members be willing to learn how to properly care for a delicate lizard?

Assess Its Health

Look closely at each gecko before you select one. Try to assess its overall health in addition to its colors and patterns. Look at the gecko's eyes. They should be bright and alert. Any sign that they are sunken indicates a dehydrated or sick animal. Any gecko kept in a cage with a sick gecko should be avoided. If one is sick, they may all be sick.

Look closely at the gecko's tail. It should be filled out and round. If the tail is flattened or has signs of the bones showing, avoid that gecko. It has not been fed enough, and sometimes these geckos do not recover. Look at where the tail joins the body. The hip area should be inspected closely. If there are any signs that the hip bones are protruding or showing, it would indicate an underfed animal.

VERIFY ITS AGE

Ask how old the gecko is. About 6 weeks should be the minimum age; between 2 months and 1 year of age is perfect. At 1 year leopard geckos are essentially adults, but will continue to grow a small amount. You will pay a higher price as the animal

approaches 1 year of age, as at this stage you can probably use it for breeding (see chapter 11 for more information on breeding your leopard geckos).

Gecko breeders and dealers are available to answer your questions.

FIND OUT HOW IT IS KEPT

Ask how the breeder is currently keeping the leopard gecko. This information is not critical, as you may keep your gecko in any of the manners outlined for you in chapter 8, but it is good to know for your own peace of mind. Being prepared when you get home with your gecko will make everything much easier. It would be best to have a terrarium set up before you shop for your gecko.

Geckos with Regrown Tails

Breeders may offer geckos with missing or regrown tails at discounted prices. Buying a gecko in this condition may or may not be for you. There are reasons to avoid a gecko missing all or part of its tail.

If you're searching for a bargain, a leopard gecko with a regrown tail is a good opportunity. The regrown tail will not look as nice as the original, but the loss of the original tail does not affect the animal's overall health.

A leopard gecko, like many other species of gecko and lizard, can lose its tail rather easily. This loss can come from rough handling, accidents or fighting with another gecko. Some large-scale dealers often buy huge numbers of geckos at one time and keep them in bins all together. This overcrowding results in tail nipping and possibly other injuries, such as missing toes or damaged skin. Breeders then sell these geckos at discounted prices. It is best to avoid this type of dealer, but, with proper care, these geckos can recover and are usually inexpensive. Sometimes geckos drop tails even with the best breeders, so do not consider a breeder inexperienced or unworthy if you see him or her offering these geckos for sale.

SIGNS OF GOOD HEALTH

The gecko you choose should be in the best of health. Here's what to look for:

- Clear eyes (free of discharge)
- Clean nostrils (free of discharge)
- Closed, clean mouth
- Well-developed body (not bony)
- Intact toes and claws (free of infection)
- Alert and active behavior

It is possible that your gecko will lose its tail once it comes home, or that your gecko's tail is actually regrown the first time you meet your pet.

DETECTING A REGROWN TAIL

The original tail is segmented and textured with a ringlike pattern to the tail tip. The regrown tail will be smooth, with no trace of the ringed texture. The overall scales will be finer as well. The color and pattern can be similar to the original or completely different. Some will even be black.

The shape of a regrown tail can vary greatly. Most will be shorter than the original and usually very stout. Some are bulbous and rounded while others may even be heart shaped. Occasionally you may see a regrown tail with two tail tips.

> ## CREATIVE ESCAPE
>
> The Texas banded gecko can sever its tail to distract a perceived threat. The portion of tail that is left behind wiggles and squirms to distract a predator, while the owner gets away and eventually grows another tail.

The location at which the tail breaks can affect the end shape. If the tail breaks near the tip, the regrown tail will be very similar in shape to the original. Unless you look closely, you may not even notice much of a difference. The closer the break occurs to the body, the more bulbous the final regrown tail can be.

IF YOUR LEOPARD GECKO LOSES ITS TAIL

If your gecko should lose its tail during its life with you, don't panic. The tail is designed to drop with minimal damage to the gecko itself. The dropped tail will wiggle where it falls. The reason for this adaptation is that, in the case of a predatory attack, the commotion of the tail will attract the predator's attention, allowing the gecko to escape. This method of escape is usually successful. Many wild-caught geckos have regrown tails, so they must have had a close call at one time.

Be sure to inspect the gecko you choose carefully before bringing it home.

Once the tail is dropped, the part that remains attached to the gecko will immediately seal itself. Fluid and blood loss will be extremely minimal. Within a very short time the wound will show the beginnings of new tail growth. A small, pointed tail tip will emerge from the middle of the wound. This tip will steadily grow away from the body and thicken. Regrown tails have a tendency to get fatter than an original tail if the owner overfeeds the animal.

chapter 8

Setting Up a Habitat
for Your
Leopard Gecko

Before coming home with a gecko, have all the supplies you need for your animal to thrive. Setups can vary greatly, depending on your personal situation. Proper setups can be visually pleasing terrariums with natural substrate (material used to cushion the bottom of a terrarium) and plants or a simple ventilated plastic sweater box with paper towel for substrate and a hide box.

Rack Units

Many gecko breeders prefer to keep their leopard geckos in sweater- or blanket-box rack units, which allow them to maximize limited space and extreme ease of maintenance. Rack units resemble a shelf unit with pull-out drawers. They are usually made of melamine-coated particle board and contain six individual sweater boxes. Each sweater-box-size unit can accommodate a single gecko or a pair of leopard geckos.

You can purchase plastic sweater-box racks from commercial sources. These racks include heat tape and preventilated boxes. A thermostat is necessary before using a rack unit to regulate the temperatures of the heat tape.

Thermostat devices can vary in complexity and expense. Some will, at very low cost, regulate one set temperature. Other thermostats are digital and have multiple settings. These units can mimic nature by slowly warming up the cage in the morning and lowering the temperatures at night.

Supply your gecko with a hiding place. Although it is safe in your home, its instincts cause it to fear predators.

Rack units require only sparse decoration. You can use paper towels for substrate. This material allows for easy cleaning; you just change the paper every two days. Natural substrates, such as sand, gravel or bark, can also be used with rack units. A hide box and water dish complete the setup. The hide box is very important. You should include one hide box for each animal. Multiple hiding areas will help minimize territory disputes by providing a secure, safe area for each specimen.

While this type of setup sounds minimal, it does fulfill the needs of this species. In order to feel comfortable, geckos need a resting place that allows them to feel secure.

Humidity

While leopard geckos come from dry areas, they spend a great deal of time below ground where

moisture is present. The increased humidity is very important when shedding. Without proper humidity the shedding process would be incomplete.

Retained patches of unshed skin can lead to the underlying skin necrosing: The underlying skin turns black and becomes infected.

Geckos need humid environments for the shedding process to be successful.

Toes can suffer greatly from incompletely shed skin. The unshed skin is like a glove that is too tight. This skin cuts off circulation and the toe will die and fall off, which can lead to a fatal infection. The humidity levels in the air can also affect long-term respiratory health.

Terrariums or Vivariums

Naturalistic terrariums or vivariums can be very pleasing in your home. They become visual centerpieces to any room. They can be custom-made out of a wood that matches your furnishings or made to fit in a room's unique space, like an unused corner. Some cabinet-type designs are made to look like antiques or are sleek and easy to clean. A vivarium can also be made from a standard 29- or 30-gallon fish aquarium.

All-glass enclosures look clean and neat and are readily available. When the right materials fill them, they look like windows into another world. Leopard geckos do very well in these types of enclosures. Some reptiles are a challenge to keep in a natural setup as they tend to be very active and can be destructive to the décor, but leopard geckos are methodical in movement and not prone to thrashing behavior.

Keep in mind that leopard geckos are nocturnal, so they will not typically be walking about during the day. Natural vivariums, or terrariums, have the advantage of looking great even when the inhabitants are hidden from view. You can, however, design your hiding areas to be up against a viewing surface; a cave that comes to the glass will give you a view of your animals while they sleep. A series of tunnels can even be constructed against the front glass surface.

You can purchase a vivarium for your gecko, or make your own if you prefer!

CREATING TUNNELS AND CAVES

You can make this type of cave or tunnel using materials from a local art-supply store's sculpture department. There are several materials available that are very much like plaster. Dyes are also available to match your substrate. If you press sand into the surface of these materials while they are still soft, the sand will adhere.

You can create very realistic surfaces using this technique. The same plaster-type material can be spread over the back wall of the terrarium to create the look of a sandstone cliff. You can make the area uneven and mold ledges. This sort of formation will allow your geckos to explore and climb.

In addition to creating ledges, you can make depressions in the ledges and outcrops for small plants. Succulents can be the finishing touch that really makes the creation look complete. (See "Adding Plants," below, for more information on safe plants for your terrarium.)

LIGHTING THE ENCLOSURE

Timing your enclosure's overhead lighting can also affect the animals' activity periods. You can set timers so the basking lights turn off at dinner time or in the evening when you may have time to enjoy watching your geckos. When the basking lights are off, leopard geckos will begin to become active while your home lights are still illuminated. This is a good time to offer your gecko food, as you will be able to watch your gecko in action. Watching a leopard gecko slowly stalk an insect can be an amazing sight.

HIDING YOUR GECKO'S HIDE BOXES

You can make hide boxes from plastic food storage containers. Quart-size containers are ideal for a single gecko. Cutting a circular silver-dollar-size hole in one side will allow the gecko access to the box. Make the hole up high on the side so that the substrate doesn't get kicked out of the box while the gecko digs. Inside should be about half filled with a medium that allows for increased humidity.

Even a plastic hide box can be part of a natural-looking enclosure. You can easily conceal hide boxes behind rocks or bark to give a perfect illusion of natural habitat, while ensuring that your animals have all they need to feel secure.

Placing the hide box toward the back of the terrarium is usually the easiest solution. Then you can build rock work or even make a cave out of sculpting materials. This way when you need to remove the box for maintenance, you can easily slip it in or out with minimal disturbance of the décor. You will need to remove the box frequently during the breeding season to remove eggs and also for regular cleaning.

CLEANING YOUR LEOPARD GECKO'S ENCLOSURE

Terrarium cleanup is fast and easy. Leopard geckos are creatures of habit and defecate in the same location. The stools are dry and very easy to collect. You can collect feces once or twice a week without the habitat developing an odor. Preventing odors is important when the vivarium occupies a living room or bedroom! An old spoon or a plastic spoon can be kept on hand to scoop out feces.

There are some plants that are safe to add to your gecko's home.

ADDING PLANTS

Décor in your gecko's terrarium can include thornless succulent plants that thrive in a dry environment, rocks, driftwood, cork bark or dried cholla wood. You can plant many species of succulents, provided they do not have spines.

Haworthia and aloe both work very well. The South African succulents called living stones are a very nice, subtle addition to your terrarium. Some succulents, like euphorbias, while thornless, may exude a toxic sap. Avoid these types of plants. While leopard geckos will not eat them, crickets might. If a cricket eats the plant and then the leopard gecko eats the cricket, you may be in for trouble.

Also avoid any spiny plants like cacti. Even though leopard geckos come from a desert environment, a cactus invites the chance of an injury.

If you choose to include living plants in your enclosure, be sure to add proper lighting. Many of these plants require high levels of light. Full spectrum flourescents often do the job. It is best to avoid placing any terrarium in a window with direct sunshine. Direct sunlight beaming in on a glass enclosure can quickly overheat and kill your gecko.

**BEWARE OF
HOT ROCKS**

"Hot rocks" are found in pet supply stores and are designed to provide reptiles with a simple way to thermoregulate. Lizards and snakes, unfortunately, don't always know when they should move away from a hot rock and have been known to burn themselves badly. Other heat sources are safer for your pet, so if you choose to include a hot rock in your gecko's enclosure, monitor the heat emitted—and your pet's behavior—very carefully.

ADDING ROCKS

When stacking rocks in your leopard gecko's vivarium, be sure to secure them in place. Gluing them together with an adhesive is a good way to prevent an accident from occurring. If rocks were to collapse, your animals could be severely injured or killed.

Epoxy or silicone works well as a glue. Both of these products are very strong, readily available and are easy to use. They do, however, require a curing time. Carefully follow the product instructions before placing them with your animals. The fumes that outgas during the curing process can be harmful to you and your animals, so make sure the curing process occurs in a well-ventilated area. Once the product has cured, the rocks are inert, safe and long lasting.

Also exercise care in placing flat rocks on a substrate like sand. Geckos can burrow under rocks, causing the rocks to collapse or fall, trapping the geckos beneath the rocks. Gluing small supports under a flat rock solves this problem. Adding these supports creates a tablelike structure, which will support the rock if the gecko's digging removes the sand underneath the rock.

Making a Terrarium from a 29-Gallon Fish Tank

A 29- or 30-gallon aquarium works well for one pair of leopard geckos. Sand substrate, stacked rocks, cork bark and a few plants can be a stunning display. To prepare a 29-gallon fish tank for your geckos you will need a few things:

- A screen lid
- A basking light
- A hide box
- Substrate
- A water dish
- A thermometer

The above list is for a basic setup that will work well. The screen lid should be an all-metal type, rather than the plastic-framed type. The plastic frame can melt under a basking light. You won't really need lid clamps, as your geckos cannot climb well and shouldn't be able to reach the top, but you should include a lid to keep hopping crickets in the cage and unwanted items out of the cage.

HEATING YOUR LEOPARD GECKO'S ENVIRONMENT

Basking Lights

Even though nocturnal geckos do not bask, overhead lighting for a heat source works well by imitating the way the sun works in nature. The overhead sun heats the ground and air, and at night, after sundown, the temperature drops. Basking lights work the same way. They have the added benefit of being very inexpensive and reliable, and they can be simple to operate.

An ordinary household incandescent bulb will work as a basking light; you need not buy an expensive reptile bulb. The wattage needed depends on the size of the cage and the temperature of the room. For a 29-gallon tank in a 70° F room, a 40- to 60-watt bulb is usually adequate for creating a warm side of about 85° F near the bulb and a cool side of about 75° F.

You should place a basking light on one side of the cage, so that your gecko can choose where it is most comfortable. If it feels cool, it can move to the warmer side. The side with the basking light will be warm, and the opposite end should be considerably cooler.

Some lizards bask; others do not.

Make a habit of checking temperatures within the terrarium on a regular basis. Placing two thermometers in the terrarium is a really good idea. One on each end of the terrarium will give you the temperature in the warm side and the cool side.

Place one thermometer in the spot on the ground under the bulb. The other should be placed on the ground in the cool end. Knowing the temperatures in these areas will allow you to adjust the light according to the temperatures in your home.

In hot summer months, if the home is not air-conditioned, the hot temperatures may force you to turn off basking lights. By placing the basking light on a timer, you can have the light turn on and off automatically. At night it is safe for the temperature in the terrarium to drop to room temperature, 68 to 72° F, provided your home isn't unusually cold.

Heat Mats

An alternative method for heating your terrarium is under-tank heat mats. These mats are placed under the bottom glass and provide a warm area for your geckos. You should place the mats, like basking lights, on one side of the tank, so that a cooler area is available.

Heat mats do not heat the air temperature of the cage, but create local warm spots. Make sure you place a thermometer on the substrate to access the temperature. You should use a thermostat with these units to avoid the mat becoming too hot. Some units contain built-in thermostats.

Building a Custom Cage

If you are handy or have a friend who is willing, you can create a cage to suit your own design or home. The possibilities are endless. You can use wood that matches your furnishings. You can create caves and tunnels that are exposed to the front glass. This exposure allows you to see your geckos while they are in their burrows, which is very rewarding if you want to see leopard geckos during the day.

Safety for your geckos is the prime concern when designing a cage. Be sure to only use safe materials and keep edges smooth. If you use wood, seal it with a nontoxic material.

If you use any silicone sealants, make sure they are properly aged before adding animals to the cage. Silicone will outgas toxic fumes while curing. This outgassing is dangerous to humans as well as animals. Make sure you glue all stacked rocks in place; digging geckos can make a pile of seemingly stable rocks tumble.

Ensure that all basking lights are out of reach of geckos. A cold gecko wanting to warm up may get too close and receive a burn. Test all heating elements to be sure they do not get too hot.

Any custom cage should meet the basic needs of the geckos. Include hiding areas and enough surface area so the cage does not overcrowd the geckos. All caging should have a top, keeping out danger as well as keeping geckos in the cage.

Leopard Geckos and Other Pets

If you have other pets, such as a cat or dog, you also need to think about keeping your leopard gecko safe from them. Do not allow your cats or dogs unsupervised access to your gecko's enclosure. A cat or dog with strong predatory instincts can make short work of a gecko. Even if your cat or dog doesn't outwardly harm the gecko, constant harassment can result in a fatal dose of stress for your lizard.

chapter 9

Feeding Your Leopard Gecko

When to Feed

In the wild, leopard geckos eat live insects, small mammals, small reptiles and small invertebrates. They remain under rocks or in holes during the day and become active at dusk. In your terrarium they will have a similar activity period. This dusk period is the best time to offer them food.

In your gecko's terrarium you can set the basking lights on a timer. Set the timer to turn off the basking lights in the early evening. As soon as the lights go off your gecko will begin its activity period. Even with your room's overhead lighting on, as long as the lighting is not extremely bright, it will appear to be dusk to your geckos.

You can sit back and watch your geckos interact, feed and explore. It is amazing how purposefully they will act. They will immediately perk

71

up when they detect an insect. They may raise up high to have a better look, and then slowly approach their prey. The tail movements during the stalking process are amazingly felinelike. The slow serpentine movement of the tail, while the gecko's body is motionless, can be hypnotic.

What to Feed

Giant meal-worms—yummy!

Leopard geckos are predominantly insectivores, but they do take small lizards, invertebrates and small mammals on occasion. For optimum health, their diet should include a variety of insects. Once in a while keepers feed their geckos baby pink mice, mostly to fatten breeding females.

The feeder items generally commercially available are the following:

- Crickets
- Meal worms
- Superworms
- Wax worms
- Butterworms
- Silk works
- Pink mice
- Commercially prepared foods

How to Feed

There are several ways to offer insects to your gecko. Some keepers drop several crickets into the cage at a regular time on designated nights. Others use feeding bowls and have food available at all times. Either method works.

One advantage of dropping in food at a given time is that you are able to watch your animal hunt its prey. The disadvantage is that any escaping insects could take up a hiding spot and remain in the cage for a very long time.

Usually insects lingering in your gecko's environment is a minor issue, but it can lead to problems for your gecko. Crickets in particular are very resourceful and hungry insects. If they should escape to an inaccessible hiding area, they may find your sleeping gecko and begin to feed on it. These bites can lead to infection and can be dangerous.

Another concern is that a hiding cricket will lose its nutritional value. Any supplement powder coating on the insects will quickly wear off. While hiding, a cricket may not have food to eat and may starve.

There are remedies for both potential hazards of crickets hiding in your gecko's environment. If you suspect a cricket is hiding in the cage, you can leave a small piece of carrot or apple for it to eat. The food tempts the cricket from its hiding spot, and the cricket will leave your gecko alone because it is busy eating. Once the cricket is out of its hiding spot, your gecko will most likely eat it.

Chow time!

Many breeders and keepers use feeding bowls to make feeding an easy task. It is best to use very smooth bowls that do not allow insects a good foothold to climb. The insects remain in the bowl for the gecko to find whenever it is hungry. The depth and size of the bowl will vary with the type of insect you offer your gecko.

It's best to feed larva-type feeder insects in bowls; mealworms and superworms are totally unable to escape from a feeding bowl. Crickets will need a slightly deeper bowl, and you may need to remove their rear hopping legs to prevent escape.

THEY MAY EAT INSECTS—BUT THEY WON'T CHEW THEM

Geckos lose their teeth throughout their lifetime, but new teeth simply grow in to replace the old ones. Most lizards, including geckos, have teeth that are cone-shaped. Unlike our teeth, lizard teeth are all the same size and shape. They will use their teeth to hold on to an insect, which they then swallow whole.

To keep insects nutritious while in the feeding bowl, keep small pieces of food in the bowl with them at all times. Cut vegetables, like carrots, work well.

Vitamins and Minerals

Supplements are very important when keeping captive reptiles. Leopard geckos are no different. Adding vitamins and minerals to a gecko's diet is very easy, and commercial supplements are readily available.

MINERALS

Minerals are the most important supplements. Calcium is the most important mineral supplement. Growing geckos need to have a regular supply of calcium to have strong bones and grow properly. Breeding females need a regular supply of calcium to develop eggs without depleting their body stores,

Even a gecko with a healthy appetite needs supplements.

including drawing from their own bones. Calcium deficiencies are common and avoidable.

You can add calcium to your gecko's diet by coating insects with a supplement prior to feeding. Insects tend to have high phosphorus levels; keeping the proper balance of calcium to phosphorus when supplementing can be tricky. Buying a calcium supplement free of phosphorus is best.

It is difficult to accurately recommend the proper frequency for coating. The most common schedule is coating every feeding for babies and growing juveniles, and once a week for adults, except breeding females. Breeding females need calcium-coated insects every feeding.

Many breeders and experienced keepers will also leave a small dish of calcium powder in the terrarium at all times. A leopard gecko will lick this powder whenever it feels it needs more calcium.

If geckos do not receive enough calcium from dustings, they may ingest substrate because calcium is in the soil in their natural habitat. For this reason, some breeders recommend that keepers avoid using sand as substrate. The ingestion of sand substrate can cause a digestive tract blockage. The advice against sand is sound, but with proper calcium supplementation it is safe to use sand as substrate. There are even commercial sands made from calcium carbonate. Ingestion of these sands is safe and will actually provide the calcium the gecko is craving. However, these sands are costly, and their benefit has not been proven.

VITAMINS

Vitamin effects and needs are not as well known in reptiles. We know that some fat-soluble vitamins

can be a problem in large doses. However, geckos need some of these same vitamins for basic life function, and deficiency can be life threatening.

Use vitamin supplements carefully. It is best to offer them, but not in the same frequency as mineral supplements. Once a week is probably more than enough, but not enough to cause a problem. Coat feeder insects with a vitamin powder on a different day than mineral powder. Some minerals and vitamins interfere with each other and block absorption.

You can sneak vitamins into your gecko's diet by sprinkling supplements on the insects it eats.

HOW TO COAT FEEDER INSECTS WITH SUPPLEMENTS

To coat your feeder insects with a supplement is easy. It basically involves shaking the insects in a container with a small amount of the supplemental powder. You can use a plastic bag, deli cup or special commercial container.

The new commercial device will probably find its way into many keepers' basic supplies. After coating the insects, you flip the container upside down to sift the excess powder from the insects. Sifting excess powder from the insects allows you to reuse powder and to offer insects without dust drifting through the air. Dust drifting through the air in a cage can be a problem. When breathed into the lungs, the fine dust can be an irritant.

HOW TO GUT LOAD CRICKETS

In order to gut load crickets, you'll need to keep them for at least twenty-four hours before you feed them to your lizard. Place the crickets in a plastic container with holes punched in the lid for air. An old margarine tub will do, or you can purchase one of the commercial cricket containers available at pet stores. Give the crickets food and a crumpled-up paper towel or section of egg carton in which to hide. Let them feast for at least an entire day before feeding them to your gecko.

Feeding crickets is not as hard as it sounds. Simply provide them with tropical fish food flakes and a slice of orange, a piece of potato or some grated carrots. Or, you can buy commercially made cricket food at your pet store, which is high in vitamins and minerals. It's important to also provide some fresh, moist fruit or vegetables for the crickets at the same time. By healthfully feeding your crickets, they will pass on these nutrients to your gecko when it consumes them.

Water

You should provide your gecko with a shallow dish of water. This practice is usually the best way to provide a leopard gecko with the moisture it requires. Some breeders have a water dish available at all times and others offer the dish twice a week. Either way is fine as long as you do not leave your geckos without water for more than a few days at a time, or forget to clean the dish after a few days.

There are many suitable types of containers that you can use as water dishes. Many reptile-industry manufacturers even make bowls that look like rock shallows in many colors to match your terrariums.

Whatever container you choose, it must meet several important criteria. The edge of the dish should not be too high. If the edge of the bowl is higher than the gecko's head, your gecko may not notice the water. Shallow, flat-bottom-type glassware about $1/2$ to $3/4$ of an inch high is perfect. The flat bottom keeps the dish stable so it will not tip over.

One of the biggest problems with water dishes is that they often trap crickets and other insects in the water, causing the insects to drown. This occurrence not only wastes the insect, but it fouls the water. You can easily avoid this problem by placing a stone, which enables crickets to climb out of the dish, in the water. You can place the stone near the bowl's edge so the insect can climb out of the dish.

KEEPING YOUR GECKO'S WATER BOWL CLEAN

Be sure to remove the bowl and thoroughly clean it every couple days to help prevent bacteria and fungus from growing in the stagnant water. For cleaning you can use a mild bleach and water mixture of one part bleach to thirty parts water.

Be sure to rinse the bowl very well. There are also several commercial cleaning products specifically made for sanitizing cages and cage materials. These products all work well and are readily available from your local pet store.

chapter 10

Keeping
Your
Leopard Gecko
Healthy

Leopard geckos can live very long lives. There are records of specimens living 25 years and still going strong. Good nutrition, proper temperatures and a good environment all contribute to the well-being of your gecko, but health problems can still occur. Preventing maladies is always easier than curing them.

Choosing a Veterinarian

It is best to pick out a veterinarian before you have a medical emergency. When considering prospective vets in your area, you should ask them several questions. Ask them if they have experience with reptiles. If they say yes, then ask if they have experience with geckos or other lizards.

The numbers of people with reptiles for pets has steadily increased, and many veterinary practices now include reptile care in their exotics departments. You can find a fairly complete listing of reptile-qualified veterinarians on-line at several locations, or by calling your local herpetological society.

If you cannot find a reptile veterinarian in your area, you might have to consider using a veterinarian near you and having him or her call in consultations to a qualified veterinarian. You might even plan ahead and ask your local veterinarian to consider expanding his or her practice.

Common Health Problems in Leopard Geckos

DIGESTIVE TRACT OBSTRUCTIONS

One of the most frequent problems in leopard geckos is a digestive tract obstruction, which occurs when a gecko eats something indigestible. This indigestible object forms a blockage that can be fatal. It can be a piece of bark, gravel or sand that the gecko unintentionally consumes while seizing a prey insect, or it can be substrate that the gecko intentionally ingested.

Calcium Deficiencies

If leopard geckos do not get enough calcium, they may eat substrate in an effort to ingest calcium. In the wild eating a calcium-rich sand can enrich their diet, but the sand in most terrariums is silica sand. This type of sand does not contain any calcium, but your gecko may ingest a substantial amount seeking the calcium it craves.

Ingesting this type of sand can form a blockage. The best way to prevent this ailment is to provide supplements of calcium. Some keepers leave a small dish of calcium in the terrarium at all times. This way the geckos have access to calcium whenever they feel the need for it. Calcium is available from many sources. Pet stores sell several brands, any of which fills your gecko's need.

If you do not want to keep a dish of calcium in your terrarium, another easy way to provide calcium is to dust your feeder insects. Place a small amount of powdered calcium (about $1/4$ teaspoon—the amount isn't critical) in a plastic bag. Place some crickets or other feeder insects in the bag with the powdered calcium. Shake the bag to coat the insects with a fine layer of the supplement.

*Young geckos
need even more
calcium than
adults.*

You may now give the insects to your gecko. You can feed coated insects about three times a week to growing geckos and once a week to adults. If you are breeding your geckos, you will need to coat the egg-laying females' insects every feeding.

When selecting supplements for your leopard gecko, do not buy a mix of minerals and vitamins. Certain minerals block the absorption of vitamins. It is best to provide some vitamins at low doses, like vitamins A, E and D. Keeping the supplements separate is the best way to regulate the exact vitamin and mineral dosages you are giving your geckos.

Most calcium supplements come with added vitamin D_3, a vitamin that is necessary for absorption of calcium. The exact amounts of vitamin D_3 that your leopard gecko needs are not known, but geckos seem to do well with a fairly low amount. Most of the commercial brands of calcium supplements provide a safe amount of this vitamin.

Calcium deficiencies can be a problem for fast-growing juvenile leopard geckos. They also occur with breeding females, who draw on their own body stores to produce eggs. The more severe symptoms of calcium deficiency include shaking or tremors and a rubbery lower jaw. If you detect the condition in time, increasing the calcium in the leopard gecko's diet can alleviate it.

Liquid neocalglucon from a pharmacy works very well for increasing the calcium levels in your gecko's diet. A very small amount goes a long way: One drop per day for a couple days, then decreasing to one drop per week, usually resolves the condition. The liquid is very sweet, and a gecko will lick the drop off the tip of its mouth readily. Consult a veterinarian to determine the proper dose, which the veterinarian calculates with the gecko's body weight.

Severe cases of calcium deficiency could have permanent effects, such as twisted limbs or other body deformations, on a gecko. Prevention is the best way to deal with this condition. Be sure to provide your gecko with enough calcium in its diet.

If you decide that a group of geckos will double your fun, take precautions to avoid gecko fights. (photo courtesy of Mark Bell)

INJURIES FROM FIGHTING

Fighting between geckos may occur if you decide to keep a group rather than a single gecko or a pair. If you do decide to keep more than one gecko in a terrarium, make sure there is only one male. Males in the same enclosure will fight.

Some breeders sell juveniles as males and females, based on the temperature at which they were incubated (you will learn more about breeding for specific sexes in chapter 11). This type of sex determination can be reliable, but only if properly done. If you do buy juvenile geckos as males and females, be sure to keep a close watch anyway. They may not turn out as expected.

Your gecko may need to visit the veterinarian once in a while.

If you are raising a pair or several juveniles together, you will need to keep checking them to watch for any fighting. If you suspect that you have more than one male, separate them immediately. If a gecko seems to hide more than the others, the others may be picking on it. Even females can have disputes. When multiple geckos are kept in the same cage, the group will have a hierarchy, or pecking order. You can reduce the chance of problems by making sure you do not overcrowd your geckos and by providing the proper number of hiding boxes.

If there is a fight between males and the result is serious, you will need to see a veterinarian as soon as possible.

PROLAPSED SEXUAL ORGANS

Prolapsed Hemipenes

Another hazard for males is a prolapsed hemipenes. The hemipenes are the internal sexual organs of the male leopard gecko. They are located behind the excretory opening, called the vent, at the tail base. Right behind the vent in adult males you will see two bulges. These bulges are the hemipenes.

Sometimes the males will evert the hemipenes, and on rare occasion one side may remain everted. A hemipenes that remains everted needs attention right away. If the organ dries out, it will necrose and need to be amputated. The reasons that a hemipenes might remain everted are unknown, but dehydration may play a part. Keep the prolapsed hemipenes moist while transporting the animal to a veterinarian. A water-based lubricant works well.

Prolapsed Reproductive Tract in Females

Although rare, a female gecko may have a prolapse of her reproductive tract. This occurrence also requires immediate veterinary care. Proper attention can correct this problem. In both cases keeping the area moist is important to prevent drying out of these internal tissues.

RUNNY OR BLOODY STOOLS

Keep an eye on the stool of your gecko. It should appear dry and well formed. It is normal for the stool to have a small white part. If the stool appears runny or has blood in it, you will need to see a veterinarian right away.

Runny or bloody stools could indicate a bacterial infection or a parasitic infestation. You should take a fresh stool sample, along with the animal, to a veterinarian for analysis. Collect the sample with a plastic spoon and place it in a plastic storage bag for sanitary transport to your veterinarian's office.

MOUTH INFECTIONS

Mouth infections can sometimes occur. An injury or perhaps an unsanitary cage is frequently the cause of these infections. Fighting between males can lead to a mouth injury. When seizing prey, a gecko may injure itself on a rock or by accidentally grabbing bark when lunging for its insect prey.

There is even a reported case of the spurs on a cricket's jumping legs causing a gecko's mouth infection. The veterinarian in this case recommended that the keeper remove the hind jumping legs of adult crickets prior to feeding them to a gecko. This practice may sound

Caring for
Your Leopard
Gecko

cruel, but the rear legs of adult crickets do pop off in a similar way to a gecko's tail. The crickets do not appear to suffer any discomfort. Pinching the fat portion of the cricket's hind leg with forceps will cause the leg to drop off the body.

The best way to spot a mouth infection is to look for swelling around the mouth area. You should be familiar with your gecko's general appearance. If there is a slight swelling, you will notice it early on and treatment can begin before the infection spreads.

If you keep a close eye on your gecko, you will be able to catch any health problems early.

Treatment usually includes cleaning the wound on a daily basis with a disinfectant and usually with oral antibiotic treatment for a specific course. For any infection, it is important that a veterinarian make a culture before treatment begins. The culture helps the veterinarian decide which antibiotic he or she should prescribe for a successful treatment. If treatment begins before the veterinarian takes a culture, the culture may not develop for the bacteria responsible, and a misdiagnosis is possible. Different bacteria require different antibiotics. The wrong antibiotic will have no effect, and your gecko may not recover.

RESPIRATORY INFECTIONS

Respiratory infections can occur if your leopard gecko's environment is too cold for prolonged periods. Watch for labored breathing or mucus bubbles on the nostrils. Raising cage temperatures often corrects the problem. If the problem persists, visit the veterinarian.

While a visit to a veterinarian can be costly, responsible health care for your gecko is important. Home care can work with minor problems, but often it does not work and geckos die. Fortunately, leopard geckos are hardy, and illness and injuries are not common. Keep your cage sanitary, feed and water your gecko properly and keep the temperatures within normal range, and you will encounter few problems.

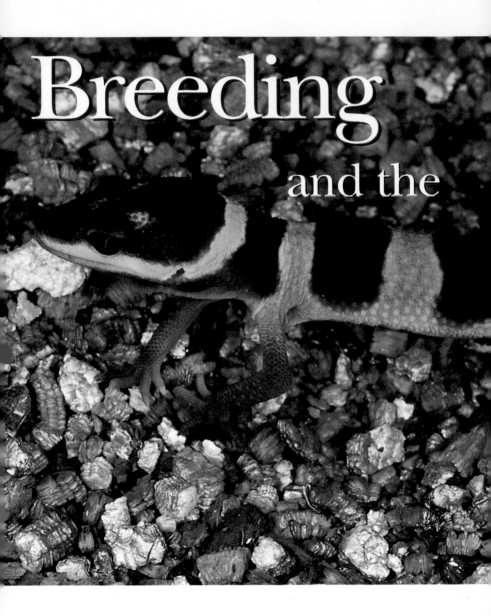

Breeding

and the

part three

Future

chapter 11

Breeding
Leopard
Geckos

Breeding leopard geckos has become a fairly standard procedure. At one time breeding any lizard was thought to be a rare achievement. Today it is commonplace that a first-time lizard breeder succeeds with leopard geckos.

Many people soon learn that having a healthy male and female in the same enclosure may be all you need to get fertile eggs. There are, however, things you can do to increase the likelihood of success.

Sexing Leopard Geckos

The most important factor in breeding is the obvious: You need a male and a female. Telling the difference between males and females can be tricky. From above males and females look alike.

CHECKING THE VENT AREA

The only way to reliably tell if a gecko is a male or female is by looking directly at the vent area of sexually mature geckos. The vent is at the tail base, on the belly side of the gecko.

Where the tail base meets the body you will see a slit that the gecko uses for defecation and for mating. Directly above the vent between the rear legs is a series of pores that make the shape of the letter "V." On female leopard geckos these pores are very small and not easily visible. Male leopard geckos have large, readily visible pores that excrete a waxlike substance.

Comparison of female vs. male gecko undersides: the male is above, the female is below.

Below the vent males have a pair of bulges. These two bulges house internally the male gecko's hemipenes. When mating, the hemipenes will be expressed externally; one side is used at a time. Comparing several geckos is the best way to see the difference, as the bulges are not huge. Once you see the difference a quick glance will be enough for you to tell a male from a female.

Handling a gecko to determine its sex can be uncomfortable for the gecko, as you must hold the gecko in a way it does not like. Turning a gecko upside down makes it feel vulnerable; it will make every attempt to right itself.

By holding your gecko you can allow it to climb over your fingers, and you can hold it up so you can view the underside clearly. Perform this handling with care. Often the gecko does not fully cooperate and the clear view may last only a second, which is often not enough time. The risk of the gecko falling or losing its tail is a concern.

It is much easier to place the gecko in a clear container, rather than hold it and try to get a clear view of its vent area. A clear plastic container, such as a deli salad container or a plastic pet cage, works well. Place the gecko in the empty container. Raise the container, so you get a clear view of the underside. Take your time and look closely; with this method you can easily determine the gecko's sex.

It is easiest to determine sex in mature geckos. Once the gecko is fully grown, all of its external features are present. The male's pores are visible immediately. It is possible to sex young geckos, but the conclusion is not reliable. A magnifying glass is helpful for determining sex in young geckos. You should examine many geckos with this method to be able to see the difference.

When determining your gecko's sex, you will find it easier for you and more comfortable for your pet if you hold the gecko in a clear plastic container rather than turn the gecko upside down.

Other external features sometimes differentiate a male from a female gecko. Males tend to be somewhat bulkier and have wider heads than females, but these differences can be subtle and are therefore unreliable.

If you purchase your gecko at a large expo or at a herpetological society meeting, you may be able to have the breeder show you the difference between the sexes with animals he or she has on hand. Seeing the difference firsthand will make things much easier.

Housing Your Leopard Geckos According to Sex

Once you have determined the sex of your geckos, you must house them accordingly. You must house males separately from one another. If not, they will fight. The loser will hide, and the dominant male will pick on him every time he tries to emerge from his hiding area. The fighting could lead to severe injury or death of the smaller gecko.

Female leopard geckos will generally get along without injuring one another, provided enough hiding areas are available and the enclosure is large enough. One male can be kept with one or more females. Some breeders keep one male with up to ten females. The best results, however, are often with one male and two females.

Raising Your Geckos to Breeding Age

The next step is raising your geckos to the right age for breeding. Leopard geckos grow fairly fast and can be mature in about one year. Males will be ready sooner than females. Females need to grow large enough to be able to handle breeding.

It is best not to breed females too young. Breeding a female gecko at too young an age could impact its growth. While females can breed at an early age, they may not be able to handle the process of laying the eggs. The eggs are large for the gecko's size and laying them can be a draining process for a young female. Most breeders wait until a female is between 18 and 24 months to breed.

It is generally best to gage a female's readiness on size and weight rather than age. Many breeders wait for a female to reach about 40 grams before considering her ready. Seasoned breeders will often wait until a female is even larger—50 to 60 grams. One ounce is about 30 grams.

To weigh a gecko a small postal scale works well. Digital scales are more accurate and give a faster reading, but they are expensive. It is not necessary to have the gecko's exact weight for the purpose of breeding. The regular small analog postal scales sold in office-supply stores will do.

Asking the breeder to determine your gecko's sex will reinforce your own findings. (Kim Bell/Mark Bell Reptiles)

You will need a small container for more active geckos. A deli cup works perfectly. Be sure to weigh the empty deli cup first and deduct that amount from the total when you add the gecko in order to calculate the weight of the gecko. A gecko's weight is very important as a way to assess readiness for breeding. If an underfed female is 18 months old, but still too small for the rigors of delivering a clutch of eggs, you should not breed her. If you are raising young geckos together and some are not growing well, separate them.

Time of Year for Breeding

The time of year also is a major factor when breeding. A winter cooldown and hibernation period usually stimulates the breeding process. During the fall when the days begin to shorten and temperatures cool is the best time to begin a cooldown.

Right before hibernation is the perfect time to offer your gecko a special treat.

It is good to give the geckos some extra food before a cooldown period takes place. Make sure they have a good fat reserve for the hibernation period. Their tails should look good and thick. Offer some favorite foods and perhaps some extra treat foods like wax moth larva

and pink mice. This extra feeding will help ensure they are in peak form prior to the rest period.

HIBERNATION PERIOD

To prepare your geckos for hibernation, it is very important to let them clean out their digestive tracts. If they have undigested food in their system when the temperatures drop, the geckos cannot digest the food and the food will rot.

In the wild when temperatures begin to drop geckos stop eating and they have empty systems by the time the weather becomes very cold. You must prepare your geckos in a similar way. When you are ready to cool them down, stop feeding them for at least a week. You should leave a water dish with fresh water, but do not offer food. Once the geckos have defecated you can begin the cooldown.

It is best to do the cooldown in stages, rather than expose your geckos to a very cold temperature all at once. A gradual shift will allow them to acclimate and naturally slow down. The first phase of cooling down can be a drop of about 10° F. Turning off the basking light and letting the terrarium reach room temperatures is one way to begin this first phase.

Make sure the temperature is just right for your gecko, especially during hibernation.

After a few days at this temperature, the geckos are ready for the next step. The second phase is to reduce the temperature another 10° F to about 60° F during the day. You can reduce the night temperature further. After a few days, you can reduce the temperature another 10° F and leave them at this temperature for about five weeks.

These weeks are a period of rest for your geckos and for you. You can renovate the caging at this time, create a new habitat or just take a break from your gecko responsibilities. The only thing you will need to do is check on them every few days to make sure they have fresh water available and that they look healthy. If they begin to look thin or are walking around a lot you may need to bring them out of hibernation early.

Finding a place for safe hibernation temperatures can be a challenge. The idea of reducing the temperatures sounds simple and the idea is simple. The hard part is the reality of being able to reduce temperatures in amounts that you can control in a heated home. Fortunately with leopard geckos there is some degree of flexibility in what temperatures will work to stimulate breeding activity.

For the first stage of cooling down, turn off the basking light or heating elements. The second stage in a heated home could be moving your geckos to an unheated basement space. These areas of most homes remain cool, often in the 60° F range, year-round. This temperature is perfect for the second stage of cooling.

The final stage of 50° F can be tricky. Some homes have an unheated crawl space in the attic or closed-off, unheated sections. You may even consider asking a friend who may have a space available.

Housing for geckos in this cool period can be very minimal. Plastic shoe boxes are well suited for this purpose. One animal per box is best, but in a pinch a pair can share a box. Paper towel on the bottom for substrate, a simple hide box and a water dish complete the furnishings. The hide box can have damp peat or moss to raise the humidity.

Pink mice are a favorite of geckos, especially females before breeding.

Even without extensive cooling leopard geckos may feel the triggers they need to successfully breed. Most breeders report more reliable success with cooling down their geckos, but breeding frequently occurs on its own.

WARM-UP PERIOD

When you remove the geckos from hibernation a gradual warm-up is best. Once their environment is up to the regular warm temperatures you may begin feeding the geckos. They should be eager to feed and will quickly become ready to mate. This time is usually good to offer pink mice, especially to the females, who need enough energy for egg laying.

Also increase the amount of calcium for females. They will be drawing heavily on their reserves to make the eggshell. If there is not enough calcium in the females' diets, they will become calcium deficient.

The Mating

The mating may or may not take place when you are able to confirm that it happens. Be sure to not interfere or interrupt the geckos during this time. The male will approach the female and typically bite her on the back of her neck. This behavior is normal, and she usually suffers no injuries. Once the male and female have lined up their vents the male will mate with the female.

As the eggs develop in the female, you will notice her weight gain. You can also see the eggs through the belly skin. The eggs will develop in pairs. Occasionally a gecko's first clutch is only one egg. Watch closely and make sure you remove the eggs from the hide box soon after the female lays them, as they can dry out quickly.

If you set up a laying box, it will be easier to see the gecko eggs.

SETTING UP A LAYING BOX

A laying box can be set up to make egg laying more noticeable to the breeder. The laying box should have the entry hole on the side of the box rather than the top. This placement will allow the female gecko to expel some of the substrate while she is digging to lay her eggs. The substrate scattered outside the entry hole is a clear sign that the female has laid her eggs. Quick harvesting of the eggs will help ensure proper incubation.

Most egg laying begins in late winter or early spring. Warming temperatures and longer daylight hours trigger mating and egg laying. The daylight hours may be the significant factor in the breeding habits of many captive geckos whose keepers do not hibernate them.

chapter 12

Incubating
Leopard Gecko
Eggs

Once you have the eggs from your leopard gecko you will need to incubate them properly to get them to successfully hatch. The process is not difficult, but can present some challenges. Watching the eggs develop and eventually hatch is a very rewarding experience.

One of the first things you may notice is that leopard gecko eggs are not rigid and hard; they differ from other gecko eggs, which are hard shelled. The eggs of Eublepharids are parchmentlike or leatherlike. The surface will give slightly to the touch.

These eggs will also expand, by the absorption of moisture through the shell, during incubation. This expansion is a fantastic process to watch. The eggs expand a very noticeable amount and towards the end seem ready to burst. Since the eggs need moisture to expand and grow, you will need to provide the right amount of moisture in the incubation medium.

Choosing an Incubation Medium

There are several incubation mediums from which to choose. The incubation medium is the material on which eggs are kept during the incubation period. Breeders have successfully used peat moss, perlite, sand and vermiculite.

Some of these gecko eggs are waiting to hatch; some have already produced babies!

VERMICULITE

Vermiculite seems to be the most reliable and easiest to use. Vermiculite is heat-treated mica. Mica is a mineral usually found in thin sheets that are very flaky.

When pieces of vermiculite are heated, they puff up and absorb large amounts of water. Since there are no organic compounds in mica, there is nothing to develop mold or fungus, making mica a very safe incubation medium. There are different size grades available. One is larger and chunkier. This grade is generally used for gardening. Another grade is fine, like a large-particle sand. Gecko breeders usually use the finer grade, but both work equally well.

You can find vermiculite at any garden center or store that sells gardening supplies. A small bag goes a long way, since you only need a handful of vermiculite for an egg-incubating container. You can add about one part water to one part vermiculite, by weight. Stir the mix well. The exact amount isn't critical. The mix should feel damp, not wet. Be sure that you cannot squeeze any water out of the mixture. If water does drip out of the mix, the mix is too wet. Add dry vermiculite to the mix until it has the proper moisture content.

The moisture content is extremely important; too much moisture can make the eggs develop fungus and too little can make the eggs dry out. Keep a close eye on the eggs and the medium. If the medium dries during the incubation you may need to add water. Add water a drop at a time.

SAND

Sand can work as an incubation medium, but is less reliable. Sand will drain water away from the eggs well, but it is harder to tell if the level is too high. In a pinch you can use sand until a better medium is available.

PEAT MOSS

Occasionally breeders use peat moss. Accessing the moisture content of peat moss can be difficult.

Choosing Containers for the Eggs

Egg containers can be many things. Clear deli cups, the same kind in which delis package potato or maca-

Deli cups make perfect containers for gecko eggs.

roni salad, are best. You can buy these containers new or recycle those you have on hand from past trips to the grocery.

Plastic food storage containers also work well, but it is best if they are clear. The clear kind allows you to see your eggs and keep an eye on them through their development without disturbing them. You can even watch for the hatching process without having to open the container and disrupt the hatchlings. Be sure the containers are clean before adding the incubation medium.

Once you have chosen a container, put about 2 to 3 inches of prepared medium inside it. Make a couple of depressions in the medium with your fingertip. The depressions should be deep enough that the eggs are about halfway buried into the mix. The top half can remain exposed.

The lid will need a couple pinholes (and no larger) for a slight air exchange. If the holes are too large, the medium can dry out. If the mix is too dry, you will notice that the eggs will begin to indent. If you catch this drying early, you can correct the moisture balance and the eggs will be fine.

Removing the Eggs from the Laying Box

One way to know when the female has laid her eggs is by looking at the hide box. At this time it might better be called a laying box. Make sure the laying box is half filled with damp, but not wet, peat moss. Damp peat moss is easy to dig in and keeps the eggs safe from drying out.

When the female digs to lay her eggs, you will see that she kicks some peat moss out of the box through the side entrance hole. This action is the sign that the female is laying or has laid her eggs. If you see the peat moss flying out or suspect she is in the process of laying, it is important not to disturb her. Once she completes the laying process you may remove the box from the terrarium and carefully look for the eggs.

If the female is still in the box carefully remove her and place her back in her cage. You can softly push aside the peat moss and gently dig for the eggs. There should be two eggs, each about 1 inch in length. It wouldn't be unusual for a first-time clutch to be one egg only. This first set or single egg might even be infertile, which would not be unusual or a sign of a problem.

If you aren't sure if the egg is good or not, incubate it anyway. Infertile eggs will begin to develop fungus within a week or so. If you see the egg begin to develop fungus, it is safe to assume the egg is not good.

Once you have uncovered the eggs, gently lift them from the laying box and transfer them to the incubation box. Some people feel safer using a spoon to lift the egg and make the transfer, but if you feel confident and are gentle, your fingers will work fine. Place the eggs into the depressions in the medium and softly close the top of the container.

Keep the eggs in a well-controlled environment to ensure healthy babies.

The eggs are now ready to incubate. Using a marker you can label the top of the container with the date the eggs were laid and from which pair of geckos, if you are breeding more than one pair. This tracking method will help you determine when the eggs will hatch and prevent you from pairing clutchmates together in the future. If you plan to sell the geckos you breed, buyers may want to know, for their breeding efforts, that they are buying different bloodlines and not related geckos.

Breeders sometimes will make a dot on the egg itself so that if someone moves the egg, he or she can place it back the way it was originally. This effort has not proved to be extremely important. Try not to handle the eggs.

Getting the Eggs to Hatch

MAINTAINING PROPER HUMIDITY LEVELS

For leopard gecko eggs to hatch, they will need some specific care. The humidity of the air surrounding the eggs is the most important factor. In the wild, leopard geckos lay their eggs deep underground. Even though the surface air may be dry, deep below the surface the soil is very damp.

The shell of Eublepharids is very leathery. This sort of surface allows for water to be absorbed through the shell. The egg will actually grow as it matures. For this reason the eggs are placed in a medium that retains humidity. Mediums for incubation can include, in order of preference, vermiculite, perlite, sand or peat moss.

If the air is too dry, water will pass out of the egg rather than into the egg. The egg will shrivel and the gecko growing within it will die. If you notice a small amount of indentation, you will need to increase the humidity immediately. Minor indentations will not have an effect on the hatchling gecko if the conditions are corrected.

If the air is too wet, the egg will develop fungus and the gecko will die. Sometimes a late-stage egg can begin to develop fungus for other, unknown, reasons. These eggs may still be viable.

If you notice a small amount of fungus beginning to grow on an egg, you may be able to save it. Gently wipe off the fungus and sprinkle an athlete's foot powder on the eggs. These powders contain a fungicide and, when used in small amounts, work without harm to the gecko. Gently dab a small amount of the powder on the egg with a cotton swab. Watch the egg carefully over the remainder of the incubation period.

AVOIDING PEST INFESTATION

Incubating leopard gecko eggs can attract flying insect pests. Very small carrion flies often become serious pests. They will lay their eggs directly on other eggs. The hatched larva will burrow into the egg and kill it. Dead eggs attract carrion flies, but the flies may attack good eggs as well. Be sure to keep incubation containers clean and free of decaying eggs or hatched eggs with possible remaining yolk sacs.

Carrion flies resemble fruit flies, but are slimmer and faster. They frequently infest cricket shipments. They live on the dead crickets. You may even find the small larvae on dead crickets, in the bedding or other material in the cricket containers.

Once established in a reptile room, carrion flies can be difficult to eliminate. Some breeders will keep flypaper in their rooms. Keeping cricket bins extremely clean will also help.

When opening cricket containers the flies will often fly out of them. Opening the cricket boxes outside will allow these flies to leave the shipment box and not enter your home. Use fresh egg cartons, as the eggs of these flies may be on the egg cartons in which crickets were shipped.

Cricket shipments may contain larvae hazardous to your gecko eggs.

It is easy to make insect-proof incubation containers. While the containers need air holes, you can use a pin to make the holes very small. Push the pin into the lid from the inside of the lid. This method makes the raised side of the hole outside the container. It will look like a funnel. The raised side is more difficult for insects to enter.

MAINTAINING PROPER TEMPERATURES

You must keep leopard gecko eggs warm if they are to hatch. There are many ways to raise the temperatures in the egg containers to the required level. If you have a warm spot in your home at about 80° F, it will provide sufficient warmth for the eggs. If you have a room for your reptiles that warms to about 80° F, you can place the egg container somewhere in the room, like on a high shelf. The night temperatures can safely drop into the 70s. For a more accurate and reliable method of temperature control you can make or buy an incubator.

Incubators

Incubating eggs in an incubator makes the process more reliable. Home temperatures can fluctuate greatly and are often too low for successful incubation. An incubator will keep the temperatures at the proper levels and even.

Commercial Incubators

Manufacturers make incubators to suit every need. You can buy a Styrofoam incubator made for classroom hatching projects for about $40. These incubators are well worth the money. There are several models available from a couple of manufacturers. The standard model will hold a couple of dozen eggs in deli cups.

Incubators help baby geckos develop.

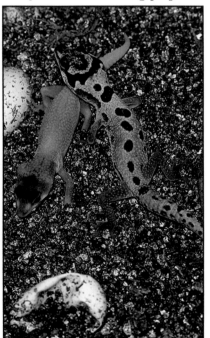

The next model above standard has a large window so you can check on your eggs without opening the unit and affecting the heat level. The top-of-the-line unit has a turbo fan built in to spread the heat evenly and reduce the likelihood of hot spots. Each unit has a waffer thermostat. These thermostats can burn out over time, so be sure to check the temperatures daily.

Set up these incubators in advance. The red light will go on when the heat element is heating. Turn the adjustment knob until the light goes off, which means the thermostat is set for room temperature. Turn the knob up in very small increments. Watch the thermometer.

Once you get to the desired temperature, leave it there. The adjustments take time as well, so set up the incubator and set a proper temperature before placing eggs inside the incubator. Any adjustment can take a while to finish leveling off. Keep the incubator in a place where the room temperatures are stable.

There are other professional breeder–style incubators available, and the prices reflect the reliability and level of materials involved. Top-level units have the ability to cool as well as heat. If you are incubating your eggs at 82° F and it is 90° in the heat of summer, only these units can keep your eggs at 82° F. This temperature regulation is very important if you expect a specific sex. (See "Incubating for Specific Sex," later in this chapter, for information on breeding specific sexes.)

Whichever incubation method you choose, a digital thermometer is a good investment. Accuracy in determining temperatures is paramount.

Homemade Incubators

Making your own incubator has several advantages. If your budget is not very big, but you do not trust your room temperatures, you can make an incubator for little money.

Old Aquariums—For many years breeders have used aquariums for incubating reptile eggs. An old aquarium and a standard aquarium heater will be sufficient in raising the temperature and keeping it steady. The aquarium will need a few inches of water to submerge the heater. The heater warms the water and the water raises the air temperature to the level you need.

Place a brick or two in the water to have a surface on which to set the deli cups. Cover the tank with plastic wrap, and you are set. You can also add some insulating material to the sides and top to make your homemade incubator more energy efficient.

You can even use the same general idea with a picnic cooler. Instead of filling the cooler with water, you can place a large jar full of water inside the cooler for the heater. This method works the same way and should be better at holding the temperature than an aquarium. If you want to get fancy, you can cut the lid and tape in place a piece of Plexiglas or glass for a window. Being able to see your eggs without opening the incubator is very handy.

Old Refrigerators—The mother of all homemade incubators is an incubator made from an old refrigerator. If you plan on having huge numbers of eggs, an old refrigerator makes an excellent incubator. It has shelving, is heavily insulated and has sealing insulated doors.

You would only need to add a thermostat and heating element. These items can be the same parts used in the classroom incubators. You can set the waffer thermostat to send power to a light bulb, or a heating cable. Mounting a digital thermometer to the outside with the sensor inside is the finishing touch.

Incubating for Specific Sex

The sex of leopard geckos is determined early in the incubation period, during the first two weeks. Temperature determines the sex of leopard geckos. In other words, the sex of gecko hatchlings depends on the temperatures of their incubation.

By regulating incubation temperatures, breeders can breed for specific sex. Buyers often request a male or female gecko. Since geckos are not visibly sexable until several months of age, regulating incubation temperatures allows breeders to sell sexed juveniles with a certain degree of accuracy. A high degree of accuracy requires extremely accurate temperature maintenance. While certain temperatures do produce females or males, there can be some geckos in the group that are not the planned sex.

Eggs incubated warmer produce higher numbers of males. As the temperature reaches a certain level the number of males increases. The higher the temperature the faster the incubation. To produce nearly all males the eggs need a constant incubation temperature of 89° F to 90° F.

As the temperature decreases the number of females will increase. To produce mostly female geckos the eggs need a constant incubation temperature of 78° F to 79° F. Temperatures below 75° F and above 95° F can be fatal to the developing geckos.

You may be able to choose the sex of your gecko before it is born if you carefully control the temperature of the unhatched eggs.

Incubating for Pigmentation

Research has shown that incubation temperature, in addition to determining the sex of geckos, affects the geckos' skin pigmentation. Cooler incubation temperatures tend to produce darker geckos. Breeders have now taken to adjusting the incubation temperatures to accommodate their needs. They adjust temperatures to produce the desired sex for the first phase of the incubation period, then reset for the desired effect on the gecko's skin pigmentation.

Candling Eggs

There is a way to check on egg development. If you feel secure picking up the eggs, you can monitor their development throughout the incubation period. This practice is called candling.

Chicken farmers developed this method years ago using candles to see if an egg was fertile and had a developing chick inside of it. For our purposes a small powerful flashlight works well. Place a small piece of aluminum foil over the end of the flashlight and tape the foil in place. Make a pinhole just large enough to allow a small direct beam of light.

By holding up the egg and placing the flashlight behind it, you can see what is in the egg. Aim the flashlight toward your face, directing the light at the egg so you can see the lit-up egg. The egg will appear to glow.

In the early stages it will appear all yellow. As the egg develops it starts to look pink; this color change is the network of capillaries spreading through the egg to provide the neonate with nourish-

If you learn to candle your gecko eggs, you will be able to track their development before they hatch.

ment. There will be a small, dark area that will grow larger over the coming weeks. This dark patch is the growing gecko. Soon enough the egg will be all dark, and the gecko will fill the egg as it completes its incubation. If the egg stays yellow it may be infertile.

Infertile eggs

Leopard gecko eggs can be infertile. It is not unusual for female geckos to develop eggs without mating. You can throw away these eggs.

Even if there were a mating, the eggs might still be infertile. You should incubate these eggs. If they are not fertile, they will develop fungus within a week to ten days. Then you should throw them away. Candling can help assess eggs, but if they develop fungus the first week, they are probably bad eggs.

It is not unusual for a young female mated for the first time to lay an infertile clutch. The second clutch is usually good. The first clutch of seasoned breeders can even be infertile. The reason is not known, but may be as simple as bad timing. The first mating may have been too early in the season.

chapter 13

Raising
Baby
Leopard
Geckos

The Hatching of the Eggs

When leopard gecko eggs are ready to hatch, you will see the eggs initially sweat. Small beads of dew will appear on the egg's surface. After the sweat, the egg will shrink down and collapse. The egg will look like it has gone bad, but it is really starting the process of hatching.

While the egg appears to collapse, the baby gecko uses its egg tooth to make a slit in the egg.

The gecko may rest and absorb the remainder of the yolk before it begins to push its way free of the egg.

Soon you will see short slits in the shell. The hatchling makes the slits using a small egg tooth on the front of its mouth. The gecko makes quick bursts of side-to-side movements with its head, slitting the eggshell with every move. The nose will emerge, and then the gecko may rest for a short period. During this time the gecko absorbs the final reserve of its yolk sac.

Once the baby geckos have walked free from the eggs and have absorbed the yolk sacs, you can safely remove them from the egg cups, although some breeders prefer to leave them in the incubation cup until they have completed their first shed. The first shed happens very soon after the gecko is free from the egg. The high humidity of the incubation cup helps make sure this shed happens in an easy manner.

The baby uses a lot of energy to break out of the egg.

Upon shedding, the newborn gecko eats the shed skin as it pulls the skin from its body, limbs and tail. Some have suggested that a gecko that does not eat its first shed does not thrive and will not survive. The shed skin is of great nutritional value and should certainly not be wasted; the skin may contain elements essential in stimulating the gecko's appetite and digestive system.

Once the baby has successfully exited the egg, you may remove it from the incubation cup, although you may prefer to wait until the baby sheds for the first time.

Sometimes a baby gecko emerges from the egg with the yolk sac still attached. There are many reasons for the yolk sac to remain attached. If two geckos hatch out at the same time, one may begin running about while the other is still in the shell. The movement of the first hatchling can stress the second hatchling and force it to flee the egg early.

Disturbing the eggs while they are hatching can also stress the gecko and cause it to try to escape a perceived predator. Hatching early causes a valuable loss of nutrients, but the gecko can do well. The best thing to do if the gecko hatches early out of fear is to leave the gecko alone so it can calm down.

Stress on Hatchlings

Hatchling leopard geckos are easily stressed. When alarmed, they will raise up on tiptoe, while arching their backs. If really scared, they may emit a hissing screech. They will usually screech if you mist them with water. The screech strongly resembles a Hollywood monster movie sound effect.

Stress has a great effect on growing geckos. Stress can darken colors, slow growth and cause aggression between geckos. Reducing stress is easy. Avoid overcrowding your young geckos by keeping a maximum of two hatchlings in a plastic shoe box. Eggs come in clutches of two, so this number of geckos per box is manageable.

If you want, you can help your baby gecko during the first shedding.

If you have one breeding pair, then you should set up a few shoe boxes to raise your young geckos. Each shoe box should contain a paper towel for substrate, a shallow water dish, a shallow food dish and a couple humid hiding spots. Small pieces of cork bark or

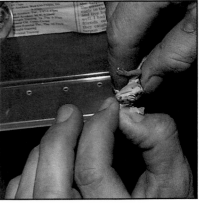

commercial caves work well. You can also use small plastic containers, as long as the hiding spot allows for a humid, dark area where each gecko can reside.

Setting Up an Environment for Raising Young Leopard Geckos

Large-scale breeders usually use larger tubs for raising young. These breeders keep many hatchlings together in a setup similar to the one described for raising one pair, but with more hiding areas. If there isn't enough food available or there aren't enough hiding areas, young geckos might nip each others' tails.

Both ways of raising young are similar and both require the addition of heating, which can range from a heated room or individually heated terrariums to professional rack units. All methods work, and the choice depends on your needs.

*A Gecko
Rearing Tray*

Rack units are shelves made to hold plastic shoe boxes or sweater boxes. The boxes pull out like drawers. Each shelf includes a strip of heating element, which heats each box on one end. One side will be warmer than the other, allowing the geckos to thermoregulate and be comfortable.

You can individually heat small aquariums or commercial, plastic, small-animal cages with overhead basking lights or heating pads. If the top is plastic, be careful with basking lights. Plastic tops can melt when a basking bulb is too close. Often low-wattage bulbs are best, such as a 40-watt standard bulb. Use a thermometer to keep track of the temperatures and make adjustments.

If you keep the room at the proper temperatures, the cages can be without heating elements, but most homes require a separate heat source for a leopard gecko. The mid-80°F range works well for raising juveniles.

As young geckos grow you can move them to larger cages. Be sure to watch the sex of geckos as they approach maturity. Separate all males and keep them alone. You can keep females in groups, as long as they have enough room and hiding areas.

part four

Resources

chapter 14

Leopard Gecko
Sources

Organizations
GECKO SOCIETIES

The Global Gecko Association is a worldwide organization based in the USA. The GGA provides a wide range of member and nonmember services. The organization's Web page is extremely useful. It provides a great deal of information and also a listserv. The listserv is a place where Internet users can post questions or participate in discussions about geckos. Anyone is welcome to join the listserv free of charge.

Membership, which does have a charge, includes newsletters and journals. The newsletters include the latest information on geckos in the world and a basic care article featuring a different species every issue. The journal *Gekko* is full color and issued twice a year.

Global Gecko Association
P.O. Box 9267
Niskayuna, NY 12309-0267
www.gekkota.com

HERPETOLOGICAL SOCIETIES

Herpetological Societies exist to help individuals, educate the public and promote conservation. All are open to membership to any person interested. Societies often provide monthly meetings, newsletters and a support network. The meetings usually feature a lecture, member socializing and often feature live animals for sale from members who are breeders.

If your area does not have a society, you may want to form one. You can accomplish this in a few ways. One would be to contact another society in your state. They may be interested in forming a local chapter in your area. If not, they may be of assistance in supplying you with information on how you can form your own society.

You could even form an informal society. This might consist of a few local people interested in holding dinners or other social events. Even small gatherings can be productive in fostering friendships and contacts and furthering the enjoyment of keeping reptiles.

Below is a partial list of herpetological societies that may interest you.

American Federation of Herpetoculturalists
P.O. Box 300067
Escondido, CA 92030-0067

American Society of Ichthyologists and Herpetologists
Florida State Museum
University of Florida
Gainesville, FL 32611

The Bay Area Amphibian and Reptile Society
Palo Alto Junior Museum
1451 Middlefield Road
Palo Alto, CA 94301
(408)450-0759

Chicago Herpetological Society
2060 North Clark Street
Chicago, IL 60614
www.chicagoherp.org

Maryland Herpetological Society
Department of Herpetology
Natural History Society of Maryland
2643 North Charles Street
Baltimore, MD 21218

The Minnesota Herpetological Society
c/o The Bell Museum of Natural History
10 Church Street SE
Minneapolis, MN 55455-0104

New England Herpetological Society
P.O. Box 1082
Boston, MA 02103
www.NEherp.com/membership.html#nf

New York Herpetological Society
P.O. Box 1245
New York, NY 10163-1245
www.nyhs.org

Northern California Herpetological Society
P.O. Box 1363
Davis, CA 95616

Philadelphia Herpetological Society
P.O. Box 52261
Philadelphia PA 19115-7261 USA
http://herpetology.com/phs.html

The Pittsburgh Herpetological Society
c/o The Pittsburgh Zoo
One Hill Road
Pittsburgh, PA 15206

Rainforest Reptile Refuge Society
1395-176 Street
Surrey, British Columbia
Canada V4P 1M7

Rhode Island Herpetological Association
547 Pleasant Valley Parkway
Providence, RI 02908
http://hometown.aol.com/RIherps/index.htm

Society for the Study of Amphibians and Reptiles
(SSAR)
Karen Teopfer, Treasurer
P.O. Box 626
Hays, KS 67601-0626

Southern New England Herpetological Association
S.N.E.H.A.
C. Baird
16 Roaring Brook Road
Chappaqua, NY 10514

Southwestern Herp Society
P.O. Box 7469
Van Nuys, CA 91409

Magazines

There are several reptile magazines. All offer a wide range of articles on varied interests. They also have extensive advertisements that can be very useful. Each magazine usually features a leopard gecko article at least once a year.

Reptile and Amphibian Magazine
TFH Publications
One TFH Plaza
Neptune City, NJ 07753

Reptiles Magazine
P.O. Box 6050
Mission Viejo, CA 92690
USA

Reptilia
Muntaner 88, 5. 1.
08011 Barcelona
Spain Tel. ++34 93 451 53 26
Reptilia@lander.es

The Vivarium
American Federation of Herpetoculturists
P.O. Box 300067
Escondido, CA 92030-0067

Books

ON LEOPARD GECKOS

The following books on leopard geckos are available. It is always a good idea to read as much as possible when researching a new animal. If you can't find one of these books at your local bookstore, check out a herp show. Herp shows are excellent resources for information on your new gecko.

Coote, Jon. *Leopard Geckos: Their Captive Husbandry & Reproduction.* Nottingham, UK: Practical Python Publications, 1993.

de Vosjoli, Philippe, Roger Klingenberg, DVM, Ron Tremper, Brian Viets. *The Leopard Gecko Manual.* Santee, CA: Advanced Vivarium Systems, 1998.

Reptile Keepers Guides: Leopard Gecko and Fat Tailed Geckos. Hauppauge, NY: R.D. Bartlett Barron's Educational Series, 1999.

ON LEOPARD GECKOS AND OTHER SPECIES

The books listed below contain information about leopard geckos, but are not exclusively devoted to one species.

Bartlett, R. D. and Patricia P. Bartlett. *Geckos.* Hauppauge, NY: Barron's Educational Series, Inc., 1995.

Daniel, J.C. *The Book of Indian Reptiles.* Oxford, England: Oxford University Press, 1992.

de Vosjoli, Phillipe. *The Lizard Keeper's Handbook.* Lakeside, CA: Advanced Vivarium Systems, 1997.

McKeown, Sean and Jim Zaworski. *General Care and Maintenance of Tokay Geckos and Related Species.* Lakeside, CA: Advanced Vivarium Systems, 1997.